Manchester United's Paul Ince gets the ball under control watched by Liverpool's Steve McMahon and Ian Rush.

PLATT'S

MAGIC

Kicked out of Manchester United at 17, his boyhood dream in tatters, David Platt relaunched his career at Crewe. His rise to fame since then has gone beyond his wildest dreams...

David won his second full cap against Brazil at Wembley.

Villa thriller David Platt has been transformed from a £200,000 player with promise to an England international with a £3 million transfer value. Here SHOOT chronicles the 'Story of a Star'.

DAVID Platt received the ultimate accolade when he was named Player of the Year by the PFA.

As one of the First Division's leading scorers and the key figure in Aston Villa's brave title bid, tributes flowed thick and fast during a remarkable season.

But it is only when that praise comes from fellow pros that a player can start to believe he has reached star status.

The fact he edged out the brilliant John Barnes and the talented Des Walker in the PFA awards spoke

volumes for his performances during the 1989-90 season.

Yet it's not too many years ago – six to be precise – that Platt was kicked out of Manchester United and told by the then manager Ron Atkinson he hadn't made the grade.

Platt was only 17 at the time and he left Old Trafford heartbroken and with his boyhood dream in tatters.

Rejection by a top club has been known to destroy lesser individuals but Platt gave an early indication of his character by relaunching his career with Crewe.

He maintains that he holds no grudge against Atkinson for his

actions at the time. In fact, Big Ron arguably did him the biggest favour possible.

Instead of toiling away aimlessly in the United youth team and reserves, forever in the shadows of Whiteside, Hughes and Co, Platt was soon to emerge as a first team player in his own right.

It was in the lower reaches of the League that he regained an appetite for the game which had left him disillusioned at 17.

Platt, born near Manchester in June, 1966, made his League debut for Crewe against Mansfield Town on January 26, 1985. In his first season he managed just five goals in 22 appearances.

In fact it wasn't until his third season at Gresty Road, home of the struggling club, that Platt began to reveal his true colours as a goalscorer.

"I enjoyed my time at Crewe because playing regular first team football enabled me to develop as a player. I probably

Continued over

PLATT'S MAGIC

progressed quicker than I would have done at United and scoring goals, albeit in the Fourth Division, helped rebuild the confidence I had lost at Old Trafford."

Even though Crewe finished in a humble 17th place in the Fourth Division during the 1986-87 season, he was the club's leading scorer with an impressive haul of 22 goals from 43 games.

And the following season, he improved on his goalscoring ratio by hitting 19 goals in 26 League games to attract a host of First and Second Division scouts to Gresty Road.

Platt decided Villa Park was the place to further his soccer education and, with Graham Taylor installed as manager that season, he couldn't have picked a better tutor.

Taylor, in his infinite wisdom, forked out £200,000 for the promising, young striker Manchester United could not accomodate – a paltry figure when you consider that, little more than two years on, Platt is valued at something in the region of £3 million.

It wasn't just the player's eye for goal which appealed to Taylor who, with his own shrewd eye for talent, recognised the enthusiasm and will-to-win United had casually overlooked. And his belief in his new signing was soon justified.

In his first 11 League games for the Birmingham club towards the end of the 1987-88 season Platt served an early warning of what lay ahead by finding the back of the net five times.

His goals on the run-in, notably the winner against Bradford in front of 36,000 adoring fans at Villa Park, helped the club clinch promotion back to the First Division.

Platt's first season in the top flight was a testing one as Villa, after a promising start, found the going tough. The club missed relegation by just one point and, despite playing in all 38 League games, Platt could muster just five goals.

Transformed

But how the fortunes of both player and club were transformed last season with Villa pushing the mighty Liverpool all the way.

And, virtually from the first game, it has been the 23-year-old Platt who has caught the attention and the imagination of fans all over the country.

Goals of every description flowed like celebration champagne from the head and feet of this impressive player who was clearly growing with confidence with every game.

By the beginning of February, Platt had already conjured up 20 goals as Villa went in search of a League and FA Cup double .

Yet, despite being in such prolific form in front of goal, Platt always maintained that he was a midfield player who derived as much pleasure from creating goals as scoring them.

In the view of many, however, Platt is not as effective as a midfield creator although his mammoth work-rate is always going to be a great asset to any side.

It is that honest endeavour – coupled with his awareness and passing ability – which has prompted comparisons with current national skipper Bryan Robson. Platt, however, insists the comparisons are unfair.

The vote of confidence he received from members of the PFA on April 1 suggests he's well on the way to establishing himself as an England star of the future.

After making three Under-21 appearances during 1988 he stepped up a grade by collecting three England B caps during the 1989 summer tour of Switzerland, Iceland and Norway.

His performances last term for Villa made it impossible for Bobby Robson to ignore him although Platt himself confesses that the prospect of playing in the World Cup finals was beyond his wildest dreams up until a few months before the end of the season.

During his first full appearance for the national squad against Brazil at Wembley, coming after a brief outing in the draw with Italy, he certainly did not look out of place.

"I thought I'd be in the B team for a while before stepping up to the full squad. Getting a call-up for the friendly with Italy came as a great surprise and being given the chance to play a full game against the Brazilians was beyond my wildest dreams."

Dreams, however, do sometimes come true ... as the one-time Old Trafford reject would now testify.

Players' Player of the Year 89-90. He forms a great partnership with Tony Daley (right).

OLD STAGERS

TOMMY Hutchison's battered and bruised legs continue to weave their magic even though the former Scottish international is now into his 40s.

The Swansea veteran sets a superb example to any youngster with designs on a lengthy career in the game.

His enthusiasm for football is undying and his attitude remains exemplory. And the same could be said of the great Peter Shilton – a World Cup star at the age of 40.

Like Hutchison he has kept himself in excellent physical shape and no doubt there are a few miles left in the record-breaking England keeper yet.

Phil Parkes, in his testimonial year, was an inspiration in West Ham's

Spotlight on the veterans who were still going strong last season

revamped line-up last season before bringing the curtain down on a distinguished career.

The likes of Trevor Francis, Jimmy Case and Ray Wilkins – who just missed out on our top 20 – continue to pass on their experience to the youngsters bidding to emulate their remarkable achievements.

Their legs may not carry them across the ground as fast as they used to but, as the saying goes, there's no substitute for experience.

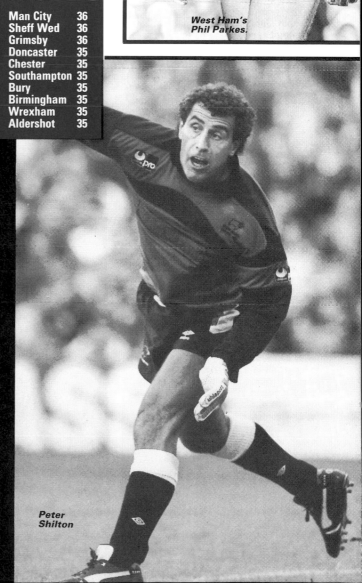

West Ham's Phil Parkes.

PLAYER	CLUB	AGE			
Tommy Hutchison	Swansea	41	Paul Cooper	Man City	36
Peter Shilton	Derby	40	Trevor Francis	Sheff Wed	36
Phil Parkes	West Ham	39	Steve Sherwood	Grimsby	36
Ian Bowyer	Hereford	38	Jack Ashurst	Doncaster	35
John Burridge	Newcastle	38	Graham Barrow	Chester	35
Kenny Swain	Crewe	38	Jimmy Case	Southampton	35
Terry Gennoe	Blackburn	37	Kenny Clements	Bury	35
Ron Hilyard	Gillingham	37	Roger Hansbury	Birmingham	35
George Wood	Cardiff	37	Joey Jones	Wrexham	35
Alan Ainscow	Blackburn	36	Steve Wignall	Aldershot	35

Tommy Hutchison

Peter Shilton

150-goal Tony reveals his...

MAGNIFICENT SEVEN

EVERTON and England striker Tony Cottee notched the 150th League and Cup goal of his career with a penalty against QPR towards the end of last season. And here the SHOOT columnist recalls some of those strikes which have given him most pleasure.

January 1, 1983
West Ham v Spurs

A dream start to my first team career and a simple goal on my League debut. Geoff Pike's free kick on the right was flicked on by my team-mate Joe Gallagher and, after Ray Clemence had tipped the ball onto the bar, I nipped in to score from the rebound.

August 27, 1988
Everton v Newcastle

To score within 34 seconds of my League debut for Everton following my £2.2m move from West Ham was unbelievable; to go on and complete a hat-trick was beyond my wildest dreams. The first one came after Graeme Sharp's shot was parried by Dave Beasant.

November 21, 1987
West Ham v Nott'm Forest

An overhead kick in a 3-2 win and arguably the most spectacular goal of my career. The second of my two goals came when Mark Ward put over a cross which I possibly should have attacked with my head. Instead, I went for glory and caught the ball full on the volley.

October 8, 1988
Everton v Southampton

We were comfortable 4-1 winners and I began the rout early on after a neat build-up involving Ian Snodin and Stuart McCall. When the ball came to me I turned Russell Osman before firing a right foot shot high into the top corner.

October 19, 1985
West Ham v Aston Villa

I scored two in a 4-0 win, the second of those being a 25-yard volley which gave Nigel Spink no chance. Steve Walford had lobbed the ball forward and I was able to turn and shoot in one movement.

Cottee is on target in his debut for Everton against Newcastle.

March 29, 1986
Chelsea v West Ham

One of the best team goals I have been a part of came during one of the most complete performances I can remember from my West Ham days. It was an end-to-end move involving myself, George Parris and Alan Dickens. George spotted my run into the box perfectly and I slid the ball home from inside the box. We went on to win 4-0.

December 3, 1988
Everton v Spurs

Not, the most spectacular goal I've ever scored but it meant a lot to me because it was my 100th in the League. I thought I was off-side as Ian Snodin played the ball in, but there was no flag and I was able to turn Terry Fenwick and find the far corner.

Ton up as Tony strikes against Tottenham.

Off the

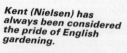

Kent (Nielsen) has always been considered the pride of English gardening.

Gordon Durie gets a few (snooker) tips off Stephen Hendry, the new world number one.

John Fashanu is directing affairs as usual.

Robert Rosario puts in some training to be Stallone's stand-in for Rocky IX.

park

David Howells and Paul Gascoigne think that Spurs should bring back their all-white kit.

Alan Smith does a bit of moonlighting, fishing the balls out of the river for Shrewsbury F.C.

Niall Quinn thinks Adrian Heath was a snip at £300,000.

Tony Agana hits the right notes with Ronnie Scott.

TAYLOR'S MASTER PLAN

G RAHAM TAYLOR has revealed his grand master plan for the future of Aston Villa by announcing that they must make the Big Five the Big Six.

Winning the League title will mean nothing to Taylor if Villa slip back to mid-table mediocrity the following season.

The straight talking Villa supremo is determined that the Midland club should now, and in the future, be able to compete on an equal footing with Liverpool, Arsenal, Spurs, Everton and Manchester United.

Consistent

Taylor says, "People have got to realise that if we are going to get this club back to a consistent level, not only I as a manager, but other people have got to look at the squad of players that we have here and improve it.

"We want to make the Big Five into the Big Six and if the players already here cannot cope with the pressure then they are at the wrong club. This was my whole purpose of coming to Aston Villa.

"The worst thing that could happen is for the club to be in the middle of the First Division. If that happens then people will walk out in droves.

"The fans are being encouraged to think that the club is on the way to the top — to stay. But we have to make sure that we have a squad of players that will be improved.

"We are not just looking at trying to win major honours. It means that we will have a squad of players that will force our main rivals to look at our squad with envy.

"If you have not got that confidence then you are a freeloader and freeloaders are no good to me now. When good players become available we will compete."

With Graham Taylor at the helm, Aston Villa appear to have all the necessary qualities to turn the Big Five into the Big Six.

Above: David Platt has made a big impact at Villa. Below: Taylor's men were pipped to the title by Liverpool last season.

YOU ARE THE REF

Compiled by STAN LOVER

1 An injured player wants to rejoin his team after treatment. Must he wait for a normal stoppage of play?

2 An attacker is in an offside position when he receives the ball from a throw-in. He scores. Is the goal allowed?

3 From a direct free-kick, the ball strikes you (the ref) and is deflected into goal. What is the correct decision?

4 A defender uses the shoulders of a team-mate to gain height to head the ball. Is this allowed?

5 A 'keeper inside his six yard box pushes an opponent with the ball. What is your decision?

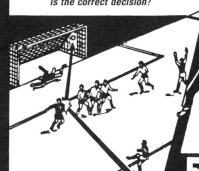

6 A player plays the ball with a sliding tackle which causes the opponent to trip over his leg. What is your decision?

1. No. He may rejoin during play after receiving a signal from the referee. 2. Yes, a player cannot be offside from a throw-in. 3. A goal. 4. No. The defender must be cautioned and penalised by an indirect free-kick. 5. A penalty-kick is the correct decision. 6. The tackle is fair because the ball was played first. Play should continue.

The ball's in Peter Shilton's safe hands.

D

o we still produce the best goalkeepers in the world?

In the 70s and early 80s, the likes of Gordon Banks, Joe Corrigan, Peter Bonetti, Ray Clemence, Peter Shilton, Pat Jennings, Phil Parkes, David Harvey etc were names to conjure with when considering who were the best shot-stoppers in the game.

But the recent World Cup in Italy made British supporters realise, more than ever, that many of the top 'keepers are now foreign.

So SHOOT asked former Arsenal and Scotland 'keeper Bob Wilson, who also wrote 'You've got to be crazy', – a fascinating insight into the history of goalkeeping – whether he agreed that there had been a shift in the balance of power in favour of foreign goalies. This is what he had to say:

"I think most people tended to underestimate foreign 'keepers because they would make a save and then perform a pirouette with a double twist afterwards. British 'keepers, on the other hand, have tended to go for safety first, never diving just for the sake of it.

"Because we see more foreign soccer on TV these days, more 'keepers with different strengths and weaknesses are brought to our attention. But overall I would agree that we are not producing as many truly consistent 'keepers as we were

Bob Wilson

WHERE'S

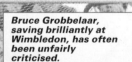

Bruce Grobbelaar, saving brilliantly at Wimbledon, has often been unfairly criticised.

in the '70's.

"And I reckon it would have been unheard of a few years ago to see three foreign 'keepers wearing the number one shirt at three big clubs, namely Hans Segers at Wimbledon, Erik Thorstvedt at Spurs and Ludek Miklosko at West Ham.

"As someone who lives and breathes my goalkeeping schools I can tell you this worries me greatly.

"For the young 'keepers already in the game however, there is a great deal to play for now. I firmly believe that Peter Shilton's crown is up for grabs. And that's a tremendous incentive to the likes of David Seaman, Dave Beasant, John Lukic, Nigel Martyn, Chris Woods, Fraser Digby and Brian Horne.

"But they should realise that time is on their side because 'keepers will often carry on playing beyond the age of 40. Take 32-year-old Bruce Grobbelaar for example. After

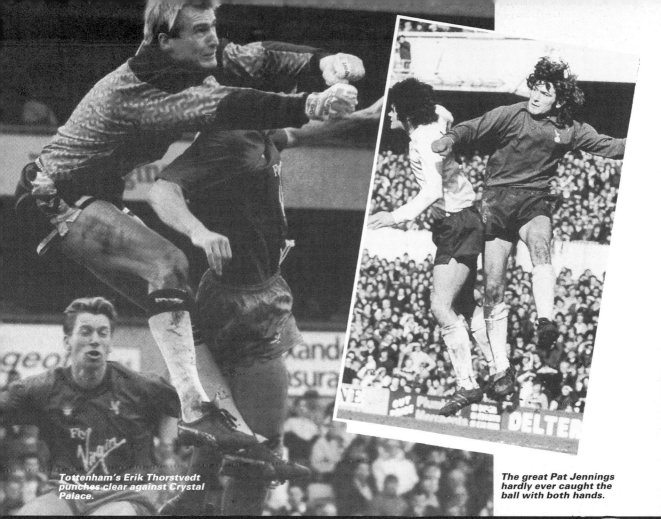

Tottenham's Erik Thorstvedt punches clear against Crystal Palace.

The great Pat Jennings hardly ever caught the ball with both hands.

THE CATCH?

Liverpool were beaten by Crystal Palace in last season's FA Cup Semi-Final some people in the media said that he might not be in goal for The Reds this season.

"I thought that was a ridiculous suggestion because, apart from judging Bruce on one game, it was

forgotten that he has such a tremendous range of goalkeeping. He actually makes other 'keepers think 'Am I doing enough?'.

"Many managers ring me up and ask me for advice on which 'keepers to keep an eye on and I can tell you for certain that given the chance about

half of the bosses in the First Division would love to sign Bruce Grobbelaar.

"On the general subject of goalkeeping I agree that 'keepers are better protected by the laws of the game these days. But set pieces have become a nightmare. Long throw-ins and near post corners are taken with the same precision as American Football moves. High crosses, however remain the most difficult to deal with as the 'keeper must judge the trajectory, pace and direction from where the ball is struck from.

"And these days the balls they use move more in the air than they use to. It will surprise a lot of people to know that my old mate Pat Jennings would only ever catch the ball in one hand because he had made an error of judgment regarding the flight of the ball. He never did it on purpose but he could pull it off because he had such huge hands, but it was always a last resort."

Crystal Palace 'keeper Nigel Martyn is a candidate for Shilton's England jersey.

SHOOT'S SOCCER

1: BECAUSE they were worried about world reaction, the design used on the first soccer stamps made very little direct reference to football. Instead it showed a winged figure which symbolized victory. Indeed, unless you were a soccer fan there was no way of knowing that these stamps had anything to do with football.

*T*HE first soccer stamps appeared in 1924, the year Uruguay set sail for Europe to take part in the Olympic Games tournament.

There had been many who doubted the wisdom of the long and expensive journey, for even their own fans felt that the South Americans would be no match for the European masters of the game.

But it was Uruguay who swept everybody else aside to take the Olympic title.

When news reached home it was suggested that such a great moment in Uruguay's history was worthy enough to be featured in the nation's postage stamps.

Not everybody was in favour of this idea, for at this time the pictures on stamps were generally limited to Heads of State or famous national monuments.

However, the wave of soccer excitement won the day, and the Uruguay Post Office issued three stamps to celebrate the victory.

These stamps are now quite rare and valuable, but since then thousands of different stamps featuring football have been issued, making this a fascinating and inexpensive hobby.

2: ITALY were hosts for the second World Cup in 1934 and they were the first nation to issue special commemorative stamps for the tournament. World Cup stamps have been released by the host nation ever since, leaving us a fascinating record of the world's greatest sporting event.

3: IN 1948 Monaco issued a set of nine stamps for the Olympics. This was the first time a major sporting occasion had been commemorated on stamps by a nation not actually

just been issued for the opening of a new stadium and one of these featured football. Spare stocks of these stamps were returned to the printers where the words 'LONDON-WEMBLEY 1953.XI.25.6:3' were added to record the date and scoreline.

staging the event. The idea was soon being copied for the World Cup. Hungary, Paraguay, Mongolia and Bulgaria were amongst the first non-host nations to issue World Cup stamps. This year over 80 countries, from Albania to Zaire, celebrated the World Cup finals in Italy.

4: IN 1953 Hungary became the first side to beat England at Wembley. The Hungarian Post Office wanted to acknowledge this defeat of the old masters, but there was no time to design and print new stamps. Fortunately a set of sport stamps had

5: THE European Cup started in 1955-56 and for the first five years the trophy was won by Real Madrid. It was then the turn of Benfica to triumph. Their victories in 1961 and 62 were acknowledged with a set of two stamps issued in 1963. With three trophies a year being competed for success in these competitions are not usually celebrated on stamps, but Poland made an exception when Gornik Zabre reached the 1970 Cup-Winners' Cup Final.

6: THE only occasion the British Post

PALBUM

Office have issued stamps with a soccer theme was when England staged the tournament in 1966. The best remembered design in the three stamp set is the 4d stamp showing three players fighting for the ball. These stamps were not placed on general sale in either Scotland or Wales.

7: BY the mid-1960s football was becoming more popular throughout the world, particulary in Africa where many nations had just gained their independence. Indeed, it is the African nations that now issue the majority of the World Cup stamps. A few sets, however, are particulary interesting.

8: BRAZIL has produced some of the world's best soccer stamps. Their most interesting issue was perhaps the victory stamps issued in 1970 to celebrate the country winning the World Cup for a record third time. There were three stamps in this set, one celebrating each of the triumphs, and each stamp showed one of the great Brazilian players.

10: MANY countries issue soccer stamps because they know they will be popular with the many people who collect sporting stamps. A good example is a set from Nicaragua. The issue was supposed to include the greatest players of all time and it is interesting to note that three of the stars – Matthews, Wright and Bobby Charlton – were English. This was because a British magazine, 'World Sports', was asked to conduct a poll amongst their readers to select the all star team. No doubt if an Italian or German magazine had been asked to stage the survey the results would be very different indeed.

9: PELE has been featured on several stamps. This stamp, issued in 1969, was to commemorate his historic 1000th goal.

empresa brasileira

de correios e telégrafos

11: IN 1982 Tanzania included a picture of Diego Maradona in their World Cup issue. It proved to be an embarrassing choice for the Argentinian star had a terrible tournament and was sent-off in the last game!

12: WITH more nations attempting to make money from soccer stamps there is a continual challenge to create designs that will appeal to collectors. Look out for collections commemorating Italia 90.

DALE GORDON
NORWICH

Shoot! SOCCER SCHOOL

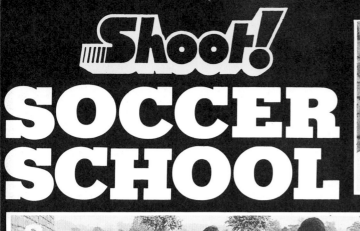

YOU, A BALL & A WALL

HOW would you like to be a top soccer star? Well, here is how to put yourself on the path to stardom, in just ten minutes a day. And you don't need team-mates, a coach or expensive equipment. All you need is you, a ball and a wall!

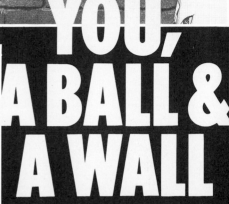

1 Alan Smith of Arsenal and former Spurs star Gary Stevens, now at Portsmouth, were once the keenest of rivals during their North London derby days. But away from the heat of battle, Gary and Alan are good friends. As our picture shows, the two stars got their heads together to plan out this super training session.

2 Firstly, practise your passing, with left and right feet. Start off near the wall and gradually work backwards. Judge the pace of your pass so that the ball comes back to you at the right speed.

3 Now let's work on your heading. Standing close to the wall, see how many times you can head the ball back to yourself, without the ball falling to the floor. It's harder than it looks!

4 Shooting and ball control. Mark an imaginary goal, by putting two markers at the foot of the wall. Now practise hitting shots into the bottom and top corners, left and right. As the ball speeds back to you, use your control to kill the ball.

5 After ten minutes of passing, heading, shooting and controlling the ball, you'll be ready for our final use of the wall. Just copy Alan and Gary. Lean back and have a rest. You deserve it!

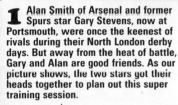

GAZZA ON GAZZA

I've always been a person who speaks his mind but, because I'm in the firing line when the snipers are out, I'm letting my football do the talking nowadays.

What I will say though is that it is my ambition, in time, to be recognised as one of the best players to come out of England. It would be a great honour to be talked about in the same vain as Kevin Keegan or Bryan Robson.

I'm well aware that Spurs fans mourned the departure of Glenn Hoddle, but he's in the past now. I am the future and I want success for the club and to be thought of as highly as him.

GAZZA ON VINNY

I shouldn't think too many people need reminding of my first meeting with Vinny Jones ... I certainly don't.

But since our controversial clash when I was at Newcastle and he was playing for Wimbledon we have become close friends – not quite as close as we were that day down at Plough Lane mind!

We share similar interests outside the game – namely shooting and fishing – and we've enjoyed a good few hours in the country over the last couple of years. He's a great laugh.

He is still a hard player though and no doubt when Spurs meet Leeds this season he'll be keen to let me know he's still around.

GAZZA'S COLUMN

GAZZA STAR

Spurs and England star Paul Gascoigne gives his views on the men he admires; those who make him laugh and those he cannot stand. It's fascinating ... it's fun ... it's Gazza - only in SHOOT.

GAZZA ON CHRIS WADDLE

I don't think it would be outrageous to say that Chris is one of the best players in the world right now. In terms of skill I would put him ahead of Diego Maradona.

I'm delighted he's done so well for Marseille but I'm sad not to be playing alongside Chris for club as well as country because he was performing at the peak of his powers when he left.

I had a lump in my throat when I heard he was going to France, but not just because I was going to miss him. I was so pleased that he'd got the dream move his talents deserve.

ZA'S GALLERY ...AND A FEW MORE BESIDES

GAZZA ON VENABLES

I have nothing but the utmost respect for Terry Venables and he is the one I have to thank most for getting me through a tortuous time at the start of my Spurs' career relatively unscathed.

He was tremendous to me and whenever he sensed things getting on top of me he pulled me to one side, had a chat for 15 minutes and got me back on my feet again.

As a player he was a bit of a character himself and I think he understands my problems better than anyone else.

GAZZA ON DARREN WOOD

He had a go at me after we'd played Sheffield Wednesday last season, saying I was too slow and I couldn't do this and couldn't do that.

Ever since then it has been my ambition to be as skilful — and as successful — as him!

GAZZA ON GULLIT

I was looking forward to playing against him during a pre-season tournament held at Wembley just after I'd joined Spurs but unfortunately the AC Milan star couldn't play because he was injured – or perhaps he didn't want me to show him up!

It would have been a good opportunity for me to compare my skills with those of arguably the world's greatest player – a title I hope to be challenging for.

QUESTION

Get together with six of your friends and play our version of Question of Sport. One of your magnificent seven will have to take over the David Coleman mantle and play quizmaster. The other six are split into two teams, A and B and are numbered from 1-3. Ready? Then on with the action…

 1

 2

 3

 4

 5

 6

PICTURE BOARD

The quizmaster covers over the pictures and gives each one a number – 1-6. Player 1 from Team A selects a number and has to identify the corresponding photo. If they answer correctly their team wins two points, if they fail it goes across to the opposition. If they answer right it's two points for them. If they fail the identity of the photo is revealed. Each player from both teams selects a photo alternately.

HOME OR AWAY?

Each player chooses a home or away question to answer. One point for correct reply to home question, two for an away one. If a player answers wrongly the question is offered to the opposition – two points are awarded if they get it right.

TEAM A
Player 1
Home: Who were the opposition when Steve Bull scored his first goal for England at senior level?
Away: Who were the first winners of the World Cup?

TEAM B
Player 1
Home: Where do Nottingham Forest play their home games?
Away: Name the three Dutch stars in AC Milan's side?

TEAM A
Player 2
Home: In what year did Tottenham last win the FA Cup?
Away: Diego Maradona played for which Spanish club?

TEAM B
Player 2
Home: How many times have Rangers won the Premier Championship under Graeme Souness?
Away: Roberto Donadoni is an international for which country?

TEAM A
Player 3
Home: Roy Wegerle left which club to join QPR last season?
Away: Which country was represented in the Final of each of the three European club competitions in 1990?

TEAM B
Player 3
Home: Who play their home games at Tannadice?
Away: Which country is hosting the 1994 World Cup finals?

MYSTERY GUEST

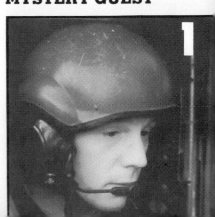 1

26

SPORT

Compiled by Steve Pearce

WHAT HAPPENED NEXT?

Team A must identify the hidden soccer personality in Picture 1. If they answer incorrectly Team B can have a go. Two points for correct reply. Then Team B tackle Picture 2.

Team A studies Picture 1 showing Bryan Robson in action and describe what follows. Team B tackle Picture 2

illustrating Diego Maradona against Brazil and describe what happened. Correct answer 2 points.

ONE MINUTE ROUND

Each team have one minute to find all nine answers. One point for each correct reply. No questions are handed over to the opposition.

TEAM A

1 Kingsley Black is an international for which country?

2 Name the three clubs Steve Bruce has played for.

3 Who won the Littlewoods Cup in 1987?

4 David Kelly left which club to join Leicester last season?

5 The following surnames could all be found in the park. Can you spot them?

a) Tim ------- (Southampton)

b) Peter ---- (Hull)

c) Paul ---- (Man. City)

TEAM B

1 Which club are nicknamed The Canaries?

2 Who headed the ball out of Andy Dibble's hands for a controversial goal last season?

3 Name the three countries Scotland were grouped with in the 1990 World Cup finals.

4 Gordon Strachan is skipper of which club?

5 The following surnames could all be found in the kitchen. Can you spot them?

a) Frankie ---- (Oldham)

b) Paul ----- (Sunderland)

c) Richard ----- (Luton)

Now total up the points to see who are the Question of Sport kings.

Answers on page 121

27

Gentle Jim aims to smash record

JIM Gallacher, the 39-year-old goalkeeper who steered the First Division part-timers of Clydebank into last season's Scottish Cup semi-finals is poised to break the Scottish League appearance record this season.

His one hope is that when he does pass the total established by Motherwell's Bob Ferrier (626), it will not be playing at Hamilton.

There is one Hamilton fan who has taken great delight in shouting abuse at Gallacher. In one match, his mother dealt with the problem by leaving her seat in the stand, and giving her son's tormentor a slap around the face.

Gallacher recalls: "That was the first time she had ever seen me play. It was the last time, too!"

Most supporters would have leapt to his defence as vigorously as she did. One reason is that Gallacher is one of Scotland's most popular pros; a mild-mannered, pleasant man renowned for his loyalty to Clydebank – this is his 18th year – and his modesty.

Clydebank coach Jim Fallon, who played with Gallacher for 15 years, says: "He actually looks embarrassed when you praise him.''

Moreover, Gallacher, balding and not particulary athletic looking, is hardly in the Peter Shilton category in terms of physical presence. "I look older than I am," he admits.

However, his appearance is deceptive and Gallacher has been looked upon as the best uncapped 'keeper in Scotland.

Jack Steedman, the Clydebank boss, and Scottish League president, recalls a conversation with Jock Stein, when Stein was in charge of the Scotland team.

He says: "Alan Rough was Scotland's first choice 'keeper then, but Jock often told me that he felt Jim was virtually on a par with him, and that Alan had the edge only because he was in the Premier Division.

"Jim himself should have been in the Premier Division a long time ago. In some ways, the fact that he is not a charismatic figure has worked against him.

"Some players with a club like Clydebank want to get away and make more money at all costs, but Jim is not like that. He is an easily contented person – he just loves to play football."

ANDY MUTCH

WOLVES

HOT STUFF FOR THE

Young sizzlers destined to be the big hits of the decade.

STUART SLATER (WEST HAM) ▶

WEST HAM'S versatile forward Stuart Slater appears to be the best prospect to emerge from Upton Park since Trevor Brooking.

His first goal for the club, in February 1989, knocked Charlton out of the Fifth Round of the FA Cup and made him an instant hero.

Slater is equally effective playing through the centre of attack or wide on the right.

His natural skills and tactical awareness enable him to create as well as score goals.

NIGEL MARTYN ▼(CRYSTAL PALACE)

CRYSTAL PALACE goalkeeper Nigel Martyn already has England Under-21 and 'B' honours. With Peter Shilton unlikely to be around for the next World Cup in 1994, Martyn will surely emerge as one of the favourites to wear the No.1 shirt.

He became the first £1 million 'keeper in British football when he signed from Bristol Rovers in November 1989, an incredible fee for a 'keeper untried at the highest level, and he repaid Steve Coppell's faith by helping Palace to reach the FA Cup Final and ensure their First Division safety.

Apart from his outstanding reflexes and agility, Martyn has the ice-cool nerves required for the big matches as he proved with an outstanding

display against Liverpool in last season's FA Cup semi-final.

He still plays with the confidence and assurance which prompted Bristol Rovers to sign him from non-League Blazey Town in July 1987 and there is no doubt he has the ability to become one of England's greatest 'keepers.

MATT LE TISSIER (SOUTHAMPTON) ▶

LAST SEASON'S PFA Young Player of the Year, Southampton's Matthew Le Tissier has established himself as one of the most promising players in the country.

His flair, pace and goalscoring instincts made his partnership with the electrifying Rod Wallace one of the most feared in the First Division last season.

He made his debut for the Saints against Tottenham in September 1986 but had to wait for Danny

90'S

Wallace's departure to Manchester United, in September 1989, before fully establishing himself in the side.

His free scoring partnership with Danny's brother Rod thrust him into the media spotlight without any ill effects last season and Bobby Robson indicated that Le Tissier will be among the front runners for England's 1994 World Cup campaign by selecting him for the England 'B' side against the Republic of Ireland in March 1990.

Southampton skipper Jimmy Case believes Le Tissier can reproduce his League form at the highest level.

TONY DALEY (ASTON VILLA) ▶

BIRMINGHAM born Tony Daley emerged as Aston Villa's most exciting player during their Championship chasing season of 1989/90.

He attended the same school as another Villa hero Gordon Cowans and signed professional forms for the club in the summer of 1985. However, his is not an overnight success story.

Only in his sixth season at Villa did Daley emerge as a player destined for international honours. He made his England 'B' debut on the same night as Le Tissier but has always shown signs of international class.

In September 1985 he marked his

England Youth team debut with two goals in a 5-0 win against Iceland.

Daley's pace and close dribbling skills can win matches on their own. He has the crowds buzzing every time he gets the ball and is now preparing to make his mark on the World stage.

KEVIN CAMPBELL ◀ (ARSENAL)

ARSENAL striker Kevin Campbell was being hailed a star even before he had kicked a ball for the first-team.

Countless goals for Arsenal's youth and reserve teams, coupled with eight goals in 14 games during a loan spell at Leyton Orient in 1989, had the Highbury faithful drooling.

His long awaited full debut came against Manchester City on March 10, 1990. A week later, against Nottingham Forest in a live TV game, he scored his first goal.

Campbell has been groomed for stardom by Arsenal's youth scheme and looks set to follow David Rocastle, Michael Thomas and Tony Adams from Arsenal's youth ranks through to international honours.

DAVID BURROWS (LIVERPOOL) ▶

DAVID Burrows spent four seasons in the West Bromwich Albion defence before joining Liverpool for £500,000 in October 1988. Two days before signing he made his England Under-21 debut, against Sweden.

He was originally signed as cover for the injured Gary Gillespie but has now emerged as an outstanding prospect in his own right. He is a fierce competitor who fears no-one in the tackle but the strength which places Burrows above the rest is his control and accurate passing ability.

Typically at Anfield, he is able to fill more than one role, and can play with equal effect in either full-back position or midfield.

Like many others who arrive at Anfield as seemingly average players, his game seems to improve weekly. He is surrounded by international experience and under Kenny Dalglish's leadership he should emerge in future England squads.

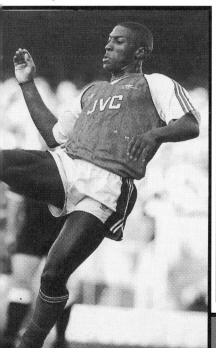

JACK IN THE BOX

ROSS JACK, the Dunfermline striker, spent much of last season at the top of the Premier Division's individual goalscorers list.

He eventually missed out on the coveted SHOOT/Adidas Golden Shoe Award, ending with 16 league goals, one less than winner John Robertson of Hearts.

Apart from the fact that he is the oldest of the top scorers, at 31, Jack was also in a team that spent most of their time battling against relegation.

Moreover, Jack scored only 31 goals in 155 league appearances for his previous clubs – Everton, Norwich, Lincoln and Dundee – and 1989-90 was only the third season in which he has reached double figures.

The other two were 1981/82, when he got ten for Norwich's Second Division promotion side, and 1988/89, when he scored 18 to help Dunfermline win the First Division title. Why did he do even better this time?

To Dunfermline's manager, Iain Munro, Jack's turning point came when he missed a first half penalty against Hearts, but scored an outstanding goal in the second half to help Dunfermline win 2-1.

"I think he has learned to come to terms with missing chances," Munro explains. "I can't recall ever working with a player who has tended to become more dejected by personal setbacks than Ross has.

Shattered

"One of the problems for us in the past is that, when Ross has not been scoring, it has affected him so badly that he has not helped the team in other ways.

"There was a good example last season, when we drew 0-0 with Aberdeen at home in the Cup. He missed two good chances and it shattered him. He was so uptight that he even missed a penalty in the replay (which Aberdeen won 3-0). From that point, Ross played as if he had the weight of the world on his shoulders."

Indeed, having scored 14 goals in Dunfermline's previous 25 league matches, Jack scored only four more in their remaining 14.

Jack, a fisherman's son from the affluent village of Avoch, near Inverness, has always had much to offer technically. He is deceptively strong for someone with such an average build (5ft 10ins, 11st 2lb). He is quick, hits the ball well with either foot and has the natural predatory instinct for snapping up goals.

At the start of his career, at Everton, he was unfortunate in having so many top players in front of him. Though he scored on his

Dunfermline boss Iain Munro

Everton debut, he spent the rest of his three-and-a-half years there in the reserves.

But there is another explanation for his failure to make an impact at Goodison. "I realise now that I could have done more in the game than I have," he admits. "I cannot blame anyone but myself."

Munro says that he has been deliberately hard on Jack. For example, when Jack's contract expired before the start of last season, he felt that his success in the First Division merited the offer of a new deal for three years.

But Dunfermline, pointing out that he had gone off the boil towards the end of the season, and had yet to prove himself in the top-flight, were only prepared to give him a two year deal.

Thus, Jack was a man with something to prove. He was also helped by operating alongside George O'Boyle and Istvan Kozma, two men with the ability to retain possession of the ball with their backs to the opposing goal and bring him into the play.

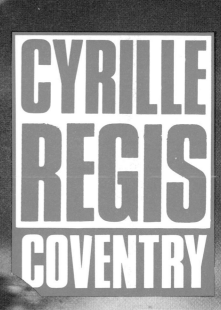

CYRILLE REGIS COVENTRY

BRAINSTORMER

CHELSEA'S Dutch defender Kenneth Monkou has hobbies that many would consider a real headache…

NOT content with a round of golf, the traditional pastime of the footballing fraternity, 25-year-old Ken is a keen student of psychology and mind development.

"I am very interested in exploring positive thinking and looking at how the brain reacts under stress, particularly amongst sportsmen. It's something that I've been reading about for some time now," he says.

"It is very important to try and broaden your horizons, to read and learn more. Having interests away from football is vital because there are times when you just need to get away from the game."

His first season in Division One was a lesson in itself following his £100,000 move from Feyenoord in March 1989. Ken experienced instant glory as Chelsea rushed headlong to the top of the table, but a succession of disastrous results in mid-season put a lot of pressure on the defence.

Meditation

However, Ken's hobbies enabled him to cope. "I'm looking into meditation as a way to help me to relax," he says.

"I've also been reading books about yoga. But I'll take that slowly because some of the pictures of the exercises look very difficult and painful."

Ken whiles away the remainder of his spare hours by listening to the soul and jazz music of George Benson and Anita Baker – he also recommends Lisa Stansfield's first album Affection.

Italian cookery is another interest and his faithful companion is an Airedale terrier, named 'Gentle'.

Kenny has been part of a Continental-inspired renaissance at the heart of the Chelsea defence.

The alliance with Norwegian Erland Johnsen formed the platform on which Chelsea challenged for a top-six placing.

"Our styles suit each other and we enjoy the partnership," says Ken. "Each player knows exactly what to do because the communication has improved and our individual roles are defined.

"We know where each other will be and can act accordingly. And the team is more compact and better organised as a result."

Ken Monkou cleverly beats Middlesbrough's Stuart Ripley in a race for the ball.

MENDER of MEN

Behind the scenes with Chelsea physio Bob Ward

THE job of a club physiotherapist is one of the most demanding and time consuming roles in a football club, but it can also be one of the most rewarding.

Chelsea physio Bob Ward admits: "It's a very intensive job. You've got to be on the ball the whole time – there's no excuse for switching off.

"There's always something to do – work at the ground, watch a match, treat players and so on. You've got to do the job properly or not at all.

"But my job satisfaction comes from seeing one of the players I have treated run on to the field fully recovered from injury."

Ward first began to appreciate the work done by a physio during his days as a goalkeeper with West Bromwich Albion, Blackpool and Wigan.

He says: "I was fortunate to spend most of my playing career under good physios like George Wright at West Brom and now I try to emulate what they did for me. It meant three-and-a-half years of training after my playing career was over, but it has been worthwhile."

His is certainly not a nine-to-five job. He says: "When there is no match

I get to the training ground about 9.30am to treat injured players with electrotherapy.

"Then the players do some rehabilitation exercises and in the afternoon we go back to Stamford Bridge for muscle strengthening routines in the multi-gym. I can be at the club until all hours.

"On the day of a home game I'll get to the ground at about 10.30am to treat the injured players. Then I'll get all my medical gear together before joining the players for a pre-match meal.

"After that, I'll go down to the dressing room and help the players with the rubbings and strappings they need for the match."

One aspect of Ward's job is to spur the players on in their efforts to get back to full fitness. He says: "On the whole, I am pretty hard to the injured players. Some need to be pushed really hard, others simply need to be eased gently along."

Not surprisingly in the world of professional football, Ward dreams of representing his country. He says: "My long-term ambition is to be England's physio but you've just got to keep working hard and hope that you'll be noticed. People talk about good work."

Ward also extends his efforts and his expertise to the rest of the local community and has set up special sports injury clinics on Monday and Thursday nights.

● *Members of the public are welcome to ring Bob and book appointments. Call him at the club on 071-385 5545.*

Bob in action at Stamford Bridge.

WINNERS!

LEE LANDS EA

United boss Alex Ferguson with the trophy.

Lee Martin scores the FA Cup Final replay winner against Crystal Palace.

GLES

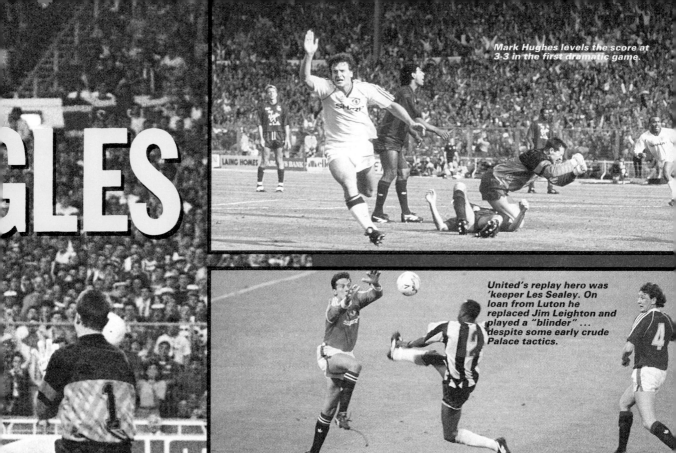

Mark Hughes levels the score at 3-3 in the first dramatic game.

United's replay hero was 'keeper Les Sealey. On loan from Luton he replaced Jim Leighton and played a "blinder" ... despite some early crude Palace tactics.

WINNERS!

WOMEN'S CUP FINAL

DONCASTER'S DAZZLING DAMES

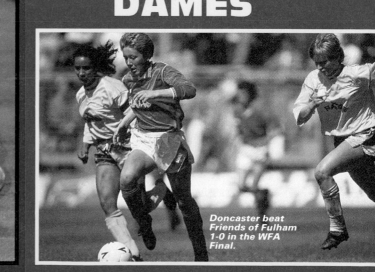

Doncaster beat Friends of Fulham 1-0 in the WFA Final.

TOP SCOTS

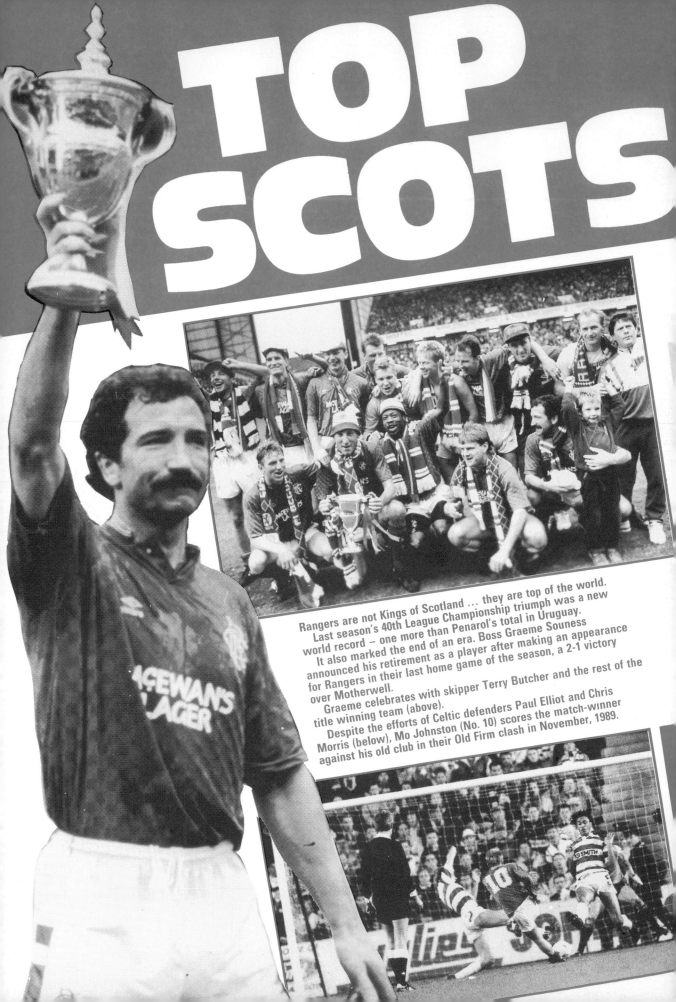

Rangers are not Kings of Scotland … they are top of the world.

Last season's 40th League Championship triumph was a new world record – one more than Penarol's total in Uruguay.

It also marked the end of an era. Boss Graeme Souness announced his retirement as a player after making an appearance for Rangers in their last home game of the season, a 2-1 victory over Motherwell.

Graeme celebrates with skipper Terry Butcher and the rest of the title winning team (above).

Despite the efforts of Celtic defenders Paul Elliot and Chris Morris (below), Mo Johnston (No. 10) scores the match-winner against his old club in their Old Firm clash in November, 1989.

Left: Mighty Mo Johnston made history when he became the first Catholic player of modern times to join Rangers.

Above: St. Johnstone manager Alex Totten with the proof of his club's success in the 1989-90 season … the Scottish B&Q First Division and Reserve League trophies.

Left: On the road back to the Premier Division Saints beat Clyde 2-0 at Firhill Park. Here striker Roddy Grant makes an effort to increase the score.

Brechin City won the B&Q Second Division last season. Here is the winning squad line-up. Back row (left to right): Steve Gillespie, Stuart Wardell, Paul Sexton, Ian G. Paterson, Paul Ritchie, Walter Scott, Gordon Lees. Middle row: Hugh Angus (assist. trainer), Robert Brown, Francis Conway, David Lawrie, Graham Hutt, Richard Baillie, Tom Gilmartin (physio). Front row: Jack Sunter (trainer), Ian Pryde, Alexander Brash, John Ritchie (manager), Chris Candlish, Hugh Hill, Richard Campbell (assist. manager).

JEMSON'S GEM

WINNERS!

**NOTTINGHAM FOREST
LITTLEWOODS CUP**

Oldham's Mike Milligan and 'keeper Andy Rhodes hold firm against Steve Hodge.

Jemson (number 10) scores the goal that retained the Littlewoods Cup for Cloughie.

Forest get that Wembley winning feeling.

Kenny Dalglish with the League Championship trophy won by Liverpool for a record 18th time.

WE ARE THE

John Barnes scores the penalty against QPR that clinched the title.

CHAMPIONS

Right: Leeds skipper Gordon Strachan receives the Second Division award.

Left: Exeter's Shaun Taylor with the Forth Division trophy.

Third Division Champions were Bristol Rovers. Skipper Vaughan Jones is now aiming for the First.

DONS

WINNERS!

Paul Mason puts Aberdeen one up in the Skol Cup Final against Rangers.

Brian Irvine scores the all-important penalty-kick decider that gave Aberdeen victory over Celtic in the Scottish Cup.

Skol Cup action with Aberdeen's Jim Bett taking on Trevor Steven and Ray Wilkins.

OUBLE ELIGHT

The Scottish Cup was decided after a dramatic and controversial penalty shoot-out after a 0-0 draw. Not that it mattered to hero Brian Irvine.

Skipper Willie Miller with the trophy after Dons' 2-1 victory.

The Dons' other Scottish Cup hero was 'keeper Theo Snelders (left) who saved the decisive spot-kick from Anton Rogan.

WINNERS!

EUR KING

SAMPDORIA: Cup-Winners' Cup.

Gianluca Vialli scores Sampdoria's second goal in the Cup-Winners' Cup Final v Anderlecht in Gothenburg.

AC captain Franco Baresi with the trophy after their 1-0 victory.

AC MILAN: European Cup.

Frank Rijkaard shoots past the Benfica defence.

Pierluigi Casiraghi of Juventus rides a tackle from Dunga of Fiorentina.

JUVENTUS: UEFA Cup.

Winning manager Dino Zoff and captain Stefano Tacconi.

David Platt, the Players Player of the Year.

Manager of the Year Kenny Dalglish with Divisional winners.

WINNERS!

There can be no finer accolade than being chosen for an award by fellow professionals or sports' writers. Here we recall the top individual trophy winners of 1989-90.

John Barnes, the Football Writer's choice as Footballer of the Year.

PFA Young Player of the Year was Southampton's Matthew Le Tissier.

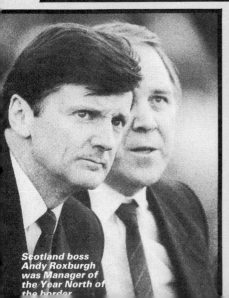

Scotland boss Andy Roxburgh was Manager of the Year North of the border.

Gary Lineker's 24 League goals for Spurs won him the Golden Shoe Award.

Left: Aberdeen's Alex McLeish, elected Scotland's Player of the Year.

GAME FOR A LAUGH

'They forgot to take the ball off my big toe'

'Are you dropping a little hint there's something wrong with my eyesight?'

'My kid brother has just found out you support Spurs. He's a West Ham fan'

'After last week's seven-nil thrashing, I thought a few flowers and things would cheer you up, boss'

'I think you must have stood in something on your way to the ground'

'Do me a favour ... cut out the sliding tackles'

GROUNDS

LET'S face it, most football fans spend as much time discussing the day they watched their team play at a particular ground as the actual stars who were playing.

And many supporters take great pride in choosing not just their favourite away ground but also what they consider to be the best designed stands and terraces around.

Here we take a look at some of those who you, the Shoot readers mention favourably the most.

A How Manchester United's famous Stretford End looked before seating was installed in the top half of the stand.

C The opening game of the 1986-87 season between Sheffield Wednesday and Everton unveiled Hillsborough's extended kop and new roof. The capacity on the terrace was enlarged to 22,000 but has been reduced following the Taylor Report.

D The Kop at Anfield has long been admired for it's singing and humour. Here the Liverpool choir are in full voice with another rendition of 'You'll never walk alone.'

E Rangers magnificent 44,500 capacity Ibrox stadium is the envy of many soccer club chairman in Britain.

FOR DISCUSSION

B Previously an open air terrace, the Clock End at Highbury now features executive boxes and a roof, reflecting Arsenal's aims to entice business party's along to N5.

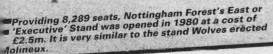

Providing 8,289 seats, Nottingham Forest's East or 'Executive' Stand was opened in 1980 at a cost of £2.5m. It is very similar to the stand Wolves erected Molineux.

G Chelsea's huge three-decked East Stand took two years to complete before being opened in August 1974, leaving the club massively in debt.

TOP TENS

Jason Dodd is finding football a 'taxing' experience.

Ten old stagers still going strong

Tommy Hutchison (Swansea) 42
Peter Shilton (Derby) 40
John Burridge (Newcastle) 38
Jimmy Case (Southampton) 36
Trevor Francis (Sheff.Wed) 36
Alan Hansen (Liverpool) 34
Tommy Tynan (Plymouth) 34
Phil Parkes (West Ham) 40
Peter Reid (Man.City) 34
Ray Wilkins (QPR) 33

Tommy Hutchison thinks over another five year contract.

Ten nicknames of well-known players

Mark 'Sparky' Hughes
Jason 'Ken' Dodd
Dave 'Lurch' Beasant
Peter 'Ceefax' Beardsley
Brian 'Choccy' McClair
Gordon 'Juke Box' Durie
Henrik 'Stan' Mortensen
Stuart 'Psycho' Pearce
John 'Tarmac' Barnes (The black Heighway)
Gary 'Bing' Crosby

David McCreery ... small chassis, big engine.

Ten tiny terrors

Danny Wallace (Man. Utd) 5ft 4ins
Terry Gibson (Wimbledon) 5ft 5ins
Micky Gynn (Coventry) 5ft 5ins
Mark Ward (Man. City) 5ft 6ins
Pat Nevin (Everton) 5ft 6ins
Kenny Sansom (QPR) 5ft 6ins
Adrian Heath (Man. City) 5ft 6ins
David McCreery (Hearts) 5ft 6ins
Russell Beardsmore (Man. Utd) 5ft 6ins
Gordon Strachan (Leeds) 5ft 6ins

Ten nicknames they never had

Inchy – Niall Quinn
Beanpole – Adrian Heath
Doris – Stuart Pearce
Ollie – Imre Varadi
Slim – Paul Gascoigne
Holmes – Dave Watson
Daniel (Day Lewis) – Nigel Winterburn
Spencer – Scott Tracey
Bathroom – John Scales
Elvis – Peter Reid

Ten goal aces who have won the PFA Player of the Year award

David Platt (Aston Villa) 1990
John Barnes (Liverpool) 1988
Mark Hughes (Man. United) 1989
Andy Gray (Aston Villa) 1977
John Wark (Ipswich) 1981
Kevin Keegan (Southampton) 1982
Kenny Dalglish (Liverpool) 1983
Ian Rush (Liverpool) 1984
Gary Lineker (Everton) 1986
Clive Allen (Spurs) 1987

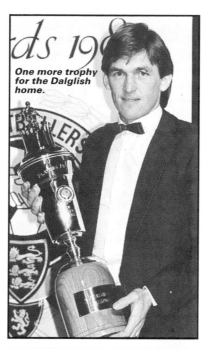

One more trophy for the Dalglish home.

Brazilian gold Careca.

Ten players who have stayed with one club throughout their careers

David O'Leary (Arsenal)
Kevin Ratcliffe (Everton)
John Bumstead (Chelsea)
Ronnie Whelan (Liverpool)
Simon Garner (Blackburn)
Kenny Mower (Walsall)
Paul McStay (Celtic)
Willie Miller (Aberdeen)
Alex McLeish (Aberdeen)
Mike Duxbury (Man. United)

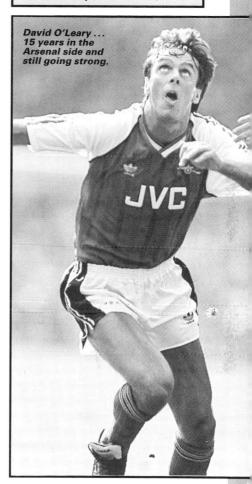

David O'Leary ... 15 years in the Arsenal side and still going strong.

Ten ridiculous club nicknames

The Trotters – Bolton
United – Cambridge/Hereford
The Haddicks – Charlton
The U's – Colchester
The Grecians – Exeter
The Gable Endies – Montrose
Cowden – Cowdenbeath
The Bully Wee – Clyde
The Baggies – West Brom
The Honest Men – Ayr

Ten players who have cost more than £2m

Diego Maradona £6,900,000
Ruud Gullit £5,500,000
Chris Waddle £4,500,000
Ian Rush £3,200,000
Karl-Heinz Rummenigge £3,000,000
Careca £2,800,000
Gary Lineker £2,750,000
Zico £2,500,000
Enzo Scifo £2,300,000
Mark Hughes £2,300,000

Motormouth John Fashanu.

Ten players who have scored four or more goals in an international

6 Joe Bambrick (Ireland) 1930
5 Malcolm Macdonald (England) 1975
5 Willie Hall (England) 1938
5 Steve Bloomer (England) 1896
5 Oliver Vaughton (England) 1882
5 Charles Heggie (Scotland) 1886
4 James Price (Wales) 1882
4 Mel Charles (Wales) 1962
4 Ian Edwards (Wales) 1978
4 Gary Lineker (England) 1987

Ten things you'd never catch these people doing

Kenny Dalglish –
hosting a game show
Tony Adams –
synchronised swimming
Stuart Pearce – ballet dancing
John Fashanu –
starring in a SILENT movie
Peter Beardsley – modelling
Paul Gascoigne –
see John Fashanu
Kevin Sheedy – playing Rambo
Peter Shilton – retiring
Jim Leighton –
wearing straight-legged trousers
John Wark –
shaving his moustache off

BEASANT

WHEREVER he goes and whatever he does throughout the rest of his career, everyone will remember Dave Beasant for his Wembley heroics which won the FA Cup for Wimbledon in 1988.

But, while Dave himself will always remember the penalty save which broke John Aldridge's heart, he is also never likely to forget an experience of a different kind from the opposite end of the emotional scale.

After signing for Wimbledon in March, 1979 — the year the club was promoted to the Third Division for the first time — he had to wait just nine months for his big chance in the senior side.

When it came — in January 12, 1980 — he was determined to make the most of it: "My League debut against Blackpool was a nightmare, an unmitigated disaster which I feared had wrecked my football career before it had begun," he now reflects with a wry smile.

Big Dave Beasant secures a place in history.

Taking up the story he recalls: "My opportunity came about because first choice keeper Ray Goddard had to cry off because of a back injury — the trouble was that I didn't know I was playing until the morning of the game.

"To make matters worse I'd spent the previous night at the cinema and capped the evening with a few beers down the pub. Although I didn't get drunk I'd had more to drink than you would normally have the night before a big game.

Erik's 'orrible debut

THERE was no prouder man inside White Hart Lane than Erik Thorstvedt as he marched out for his Tottenham debut.

But there probably wasn't a more disconsolate figure in the whole of North London at the end of a nightmare 90 minutes for the giant Norwegian.

He made the worst possible start to his Spurs career by letting a tame Nigel Clough shot slip though is fingers — in front of the TV cameras too.

Thorstvedt doesn't need reminding of the incident which haunted him for weeks. Neither has he forgotten some of the cruel jibes which welcomed him to the cut and thrust world of English football.

'Erik the 'Orrible' had arrived ... and boy did he know it.

Now though, having established himself as Spurs number one keeper and a big favourite with the White Hart Lane crowd, he can afford to look back with a grin not a grimace.

"It wasn't quite the impression I'd

I feared I'd blown it

"When Ray phoned me at home in the morning to say he was struggling and that I would be in the team my first thoughts were 'oh no, I shouldn't have had those beers last night'.

"When the game was over and I was sitting in the dressing room brooding about Blackpool's winning goal which I'd let through my legs I vowed never to drink again before a match.

"I put my mistake, an elementary keeper's error, down to my poor preparation and following our 2-1 defeat in front of our own fans too — I was virtually inconsolable. All sorts of desperate thoughts were racing through my mind, not least the fear that I'd blown my big chance."

When manager Dario Gradi instructed his number two Dave Bassett to begin an instant search for a new keeper, the boy Beasant's worst fears looked like being realised.

But, mainly thanks to the persuasive tongue of Harry Bassett, Wimbledon kept faith with their young stopper. The rest, as they say, is history.

hoped to make," he laughs, "and I'd be lying if I said I wasn't affected by that mistake.

"It was a nerve-racking time for me but I was determined that I wasn't going to lose my confidence over one incident. If a keeper loses his confidence, he loses everything.

"Fortunately I managed to pull through it and by doing so I have become tougher mentally and, hopefully, a better keeper."

There is no doubt that Erik has since won over the Spurs fans — and kept the soccer cynics at bay — with his performances for club and country. It didn't happen overnight, however.

"It wasn't until we beat Nottingham Forest in the return a couple of months later that I felt I had put the records straight," recalls the friendly viking.

Yet for all his stunning performances for Spurs since, he has been unable to inspire them to trophy success of any kind. He hopes to put that right during the 1990-91 season.

Scotland's is top-

McDairmid Park, St. Johnstone's magnificent all-purpose stadium.

Alex Totton

Partick's Chic Charnley has set a fine example on the field.

ANYTHING you can do, we can do better seems to be the call of clubs outside Scotland's glamour league.

Teams such as Partick Thistle, Airdrie and Falkirk are no longer content to play second fiddle to the big guns of the Premier League.

With proposals being put forward every other month of reconstruction, the clubs in the First Division are making sure that should anything come out of these plans, they will be more than well prepared for the leap into the top league.

Football in the First Division is booming; and with more and more business men coming into the game, the challenge for them is to emulate the feats of what's going on at Ibrox.

Perth club St. Johnstone, promoted to the Premier last season, led the way, with their brand new 10,000 all

First class

Partick (stripes) and Airdrie are just two of the progressive clubs looking to the future.

Thistle 'keeper Cammy Duncan has had experience at top level.

seater stadium, named McDairmid Park, after a local farmer who donated the land.

The stadium is on three levels and also has its own artificial pitch alongside the main stadium. There are four sets of changing rooms, a gymnasium and business offices.

During the week the club opens it's doors to the public in offering bar lunches and a host of other activities.

Manager Alex Totten has led the way in transfer fees also, by paying a club record of £80,000 for Hearts winger Alan Moore, £50,000 to Dundee United for midfielder Harry Curran and £30,000 to Clydebank for defender Mark Treanor.

Crowds have trebled and the club is gearing itself for a long stay in the Premier League.

Centre-half Paul Cherry says: "The place is buzzing. The atmosphere in the ground has been electric at times and some of our matches have had to be all ticket affairs."

Over in Glasgow, Partick Thistle are wowing the fans and bringing the sunshine days back to Firhill.

Cheeky Chic Charnley and his troops are leading the way on the field and there are plans afoot to turn Firhill into a new £5 million super stadium.

Man at the helm is Thistle boss

John Lambie who has already steered Hamilton twice to promotion to the Premier League. He has gone for experienced players in his bid to get the Jags back into the top flight.

Players such as Roddie MacDonald, Brian Wright, Alex Kennedy, Charlie Adam and £60,000 acquisition from Motherwell, goalkeeper Cammy Duncan, have all played at the top level and know what's needed in the months that lie ahead.

Down in Broomfield, home of Airdrie, Jimmy Bone has his team fired up in their quest for Premier League glory.

Having sold top goalscorer Kenny MacDonald to Raith Rovers for £80,000 he immediately went out and purchased Graham Harvey from Dundee who settled in straight away by scoring against Clydebank on his debut.

Whatever happens in Scottish Football this year, whether reconstruction takes place or not, the First Division clubs in Scotland will be prepared for any challenge.

1 His Christian name isn't really Roy Aitken. The names on his birth certificate are Robert Sime Aitken.

2 He joined the Parkhead side as a schoolboy in 1974 from Celtic Boys Club and former boss Jock Stein earmarked him at the time as "a star of the future".

3 Jock Stein drafted the young, but powerful Aitken into the Celtic first team when he was just 16. He made his debut in a League Cup tie at Stenhousemuir in 1975.

4 Because he was still at school, Roy (then 17) had to apply for permission to fly with Celtic for a Cup Winners Cup clash with Zwickau of East Germany. The school agreed providing Celtic acted as his 'parents' for the trip.

5 He was known as 'The Bear' to Celtic fans for his driving runs from defence, and his booming voice also became a trademark for the player who was a natural leader.

10 THINGS YOU NEVER KNEW ABOUT ROY AITKEN

6 He only graduated to skipper of Celtic in 1987 when Danny McGrain retired. He became Scotland captain in the same year.

7 Although he had his critics, defensively at least, over 40,000 fans turned out to pay tribute in his testimonial match against Manchester United in March, 1987.

8 Roy, a teetotal, family man with two children – Ashley (9) and John (7) – is a first-rate classical pianist.

9 Before committing himself to a career in football, Roy was a highly-rated basketball player and led his school, St. Andrews, Saltcoats, to the Scottish Schools Basketball Cup. He was also selected to play for his country.

10 In 17 years at Parkhead he won six League Championship medals (including two League and Cup doubles), five Scottish Cup winners medals and a Skol Cup winners medal. He has over 50 Scotland caps. He was transferred to Newcastle United in January 1990 for £500,000.

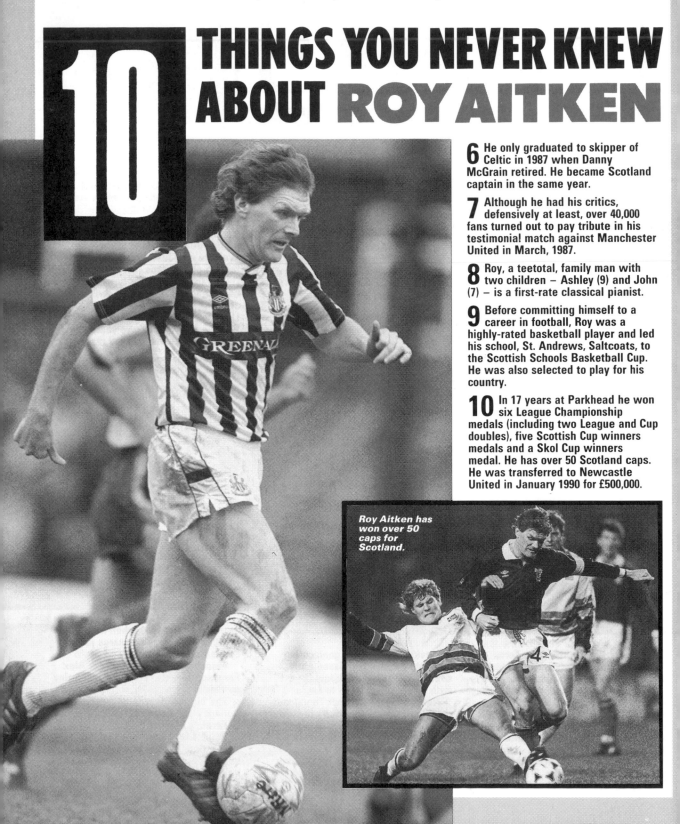

Roy Aitken has won over 50 caps for Scotland.

ON

TONY CASCARINO

(Aston Villa and Rep. of Ireland)

FULL NAME: Anthony Cascarino
BIRTHPLACE: St.Paul's Cray, London.
DATE OF BIRTH: September 1, 1962.
MARRIED: Yes, to Sarah.
CHILDREN: One son, Michael.
CLUBS TO DATE: Gillingham, Millwall and Aston Villa.
INTERNATIONAL DEBUT: (for Eire) v Switzerland, 1985.

HOW DID YOU BREAK INTO LEAGUE FOOTBALL?
teenager I was working in the building trade and playing for a team called Crockenhill in the Kent League. Our sponge man, Peter Willard, mentioned me to his brother-in-law who turned out to be Gillingham boss Keith Peacock. I think Peter told him to come and have a look at me and the whole thing blossomed from there. The transfer fee was something like a set of tracksuits.

HAD YOU HAD TRIALS FOR ANY TEAMS BEFORE SIGNING FOR GILLINGHAM? After playing for Kent Schools I did have trials for QPR and also went to Charlton for a while. But neither club was prepared to take me on and, when I left school, I gave up the game for a couple of years because I had to work on Saturdays.

DID YOU ENJOY YOUR TIME AT GILLINGHAM? Yes, I loved every minute of my five and a half years there … well almost every minute. Losing out to Swindon in the promotion play-offs in 1987, after scoring a hat-trick against Sunderland to put us in the Final, was a massive disappointment. I scored over 100 League and Cup goals for Gillingham, but my one regret was that we never got promoted.

WHAT WAS IT LIKE PLAYING FOR THE SO-CALLED 'HEAD CASES' OF MILLWALL? It was great, especially winning a Second Division Championship winners' medal at the end of my first season in 1988. Our first year in Division One was pretty good too and I think we took a few people by surprise. When there was a battle to be won, we won it – and

nine times out of ten, we won the game.

WAS IT DIFFICULT LEAVING MILLWALL KNOWING THEY WERE IN SUCH DESPERATE TROUBLE LAST SEASON? as hard a decision as I have had to face in football. I didn't want people to think I was going because we were in a bad position at the foot of the table, but the opportunity to join Villa was one I couldn't refuse. I had to take a bit of stick from my mates about leaving though. I'm just sorry Millwall couldn't avoid the drop back into Division Two.

WAS IT A SURPRISE TO GET A CALL-UP FOR THE REPUBLIC OF IRELAND SQUAD? Gillingham my team-mate Seamus McDonough – Eire's 'keeper – asked me if I had any Irish qualification. I told him that I had Irish grandparents on my mother's side and he mentioned it to the Republic boss at the time, Eoin Hand. One thing led to another and by the start of the 1985-86 season I was in the squad. You could say it's gone pretty well since.

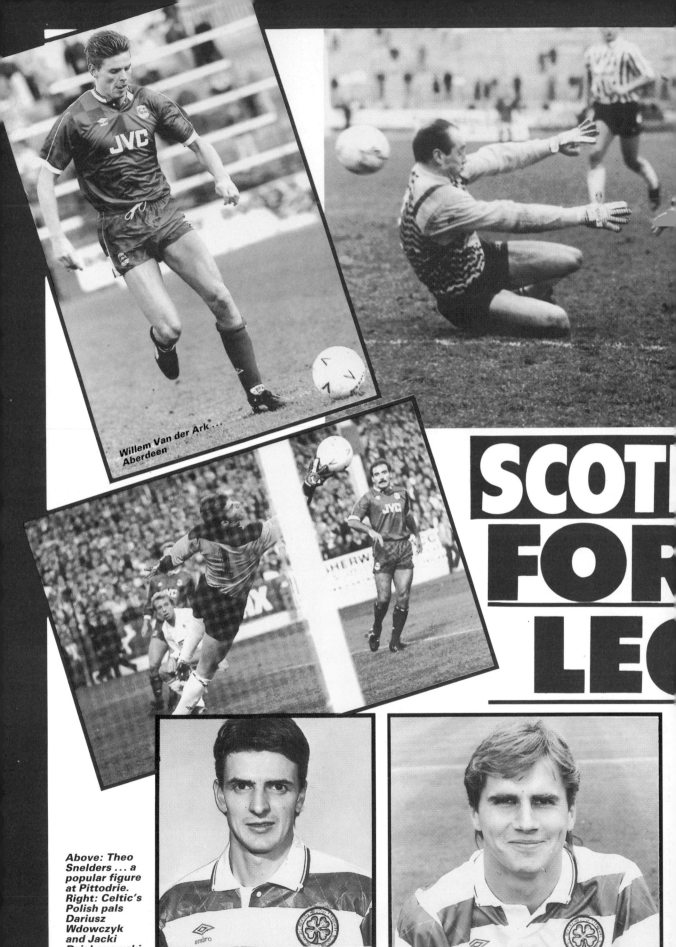

Willem Van der Ark ...
Aberdeen

SCOT
FOR
LEG

Above: Theo
Snelders ... a
popular figure
at Pittodrie.
Right: Celtic's
Polish pals
Dariusz
Wdowczyk
and Jacki
Dziekanowski.

Aberdeen's Dutch striker Hans Gillhaus scores against Dunfermline.

Gudmunder Torfason clears for St Mirren v Rangers.

AND'S EIGN ION

SCOTLAND'S bosses showed real taste when they opted for the Continental flavour.

Top of the menu are Aberdeen's Dutch double act Theo Snelders and Hans Gillhaus whose influence was considerable in steering The Dons to Scottish Cup and Skol Cup glory last season.

Goalkeeper Snelders is now rated as one of the best in Europe while Gillhaus, a £650,000 buy from PSV Eindhoven, has shown lethal striking form which earned him a spot in Holland's World Cup squad in Italy.

Pittodrie boss Alex Smith also has another Dutchman to call on in 6ft 5in beanpole forward Willem Van der Ark.

One of the other big successes in the Foreign Legion has been St Mirren's Gudmunder Torfason. The big Icelandic striker arrived from Austrian club Rapid Vienna for £200,000 but became one of Scotland's top scorers and now has a £1million price tag.

The Iceman has continental company at Paisley in German ace Tomas Stickroth, a George Michael lookalike, who cost £400,000 from Bundesliga club Bayer Uerdigen.

Celtic went for an Eastern block booking when they snapped up Polish pals Jacki Dziekanowski and Dariusz Wdowczyk from Legia Warsaw in a £1million deal.

Jacki, especially, became the darling of the Parkhead fans with some sizzling goals and caught the eye as one of the most skilful players around along with Dunfermline's very talented Hungarian Istvan Kozma, who was bought from French club Bordeaux for £300,000.

Dundee United have a real cosmopolitan look with Yugoslav Miodrag Krivokapic, Finnish striker Mixu Paatelainen and last season's buy from Holland, hard man Freddy Van der Hoorn. Freddy was a snip at £200,000 and had a good enough season to suggest he'll be at Tannadice for some time to come.

Champions Rangers, brought Israeli keeper Bonni Ginburg to Ibrox as deputy for Chris Woods, but the costly experience of Hearts into the Euro market last season suggests that caution is necessary.

They forked out £200,000 for Yugoslav striker Husref Musemic from Red Star Belgrade but he flopped and the Edinburgh club got rid of him five months later for nothing.

Husref Musemic of Hearts.

Dundee United's Freddy Van der Hoorn.

Putting on the

Who said Barnsley don't have any stars these days?

As styles of play have changed dramatically through the years, so too have the kits worn by your soccer heroes. And not always for the better!

Just look at some of the hideous outfits that have cropped up since the Seventies, when kit manufacturers realised that every schoolboy in the land wanted the chance to look like their Saturday idols.

From Leeds United's trend-setting number tags stuck in their socks, to Manchester City's infamous checks and Barnsley's latest star-infested effort, football kits have never failed to provide us with the odd giggle.

Football these days is like a game of chess according to three Manchester City defenders who've brought along their own boards.

Style

Peter Shilton models the latest collection from Umbro's 'On Safari' range.

Now you know the real reason why Gary Pallister couldn't get away from Middlesbrough quickly enough.

Don Revie looks on approvingly at Billy Bremner's number tags.

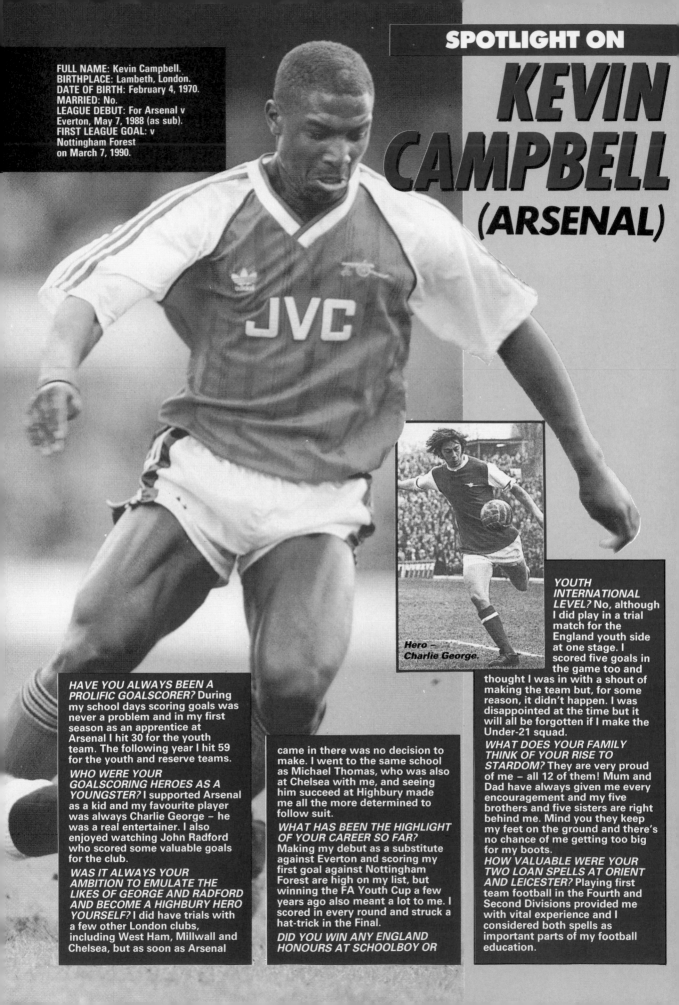

KEVIN CAMPBELL
(ARSENAL)

FULL NAME: Kevin Campbell.
BIRTHPLACE: Lambeth, London.
DATE OF BIRTH: February 4, 1970.
MARRIED: No.
LEAGUE DEBUT: For Arsenal v Everton, May 7, 1988 (as sub).
FIRST LEAGUE GOAL: v Nottingham Forest on March 7, 1990.

Hero – Charlie George.

HAVE YOU ALWAYS BEEN A PROLIFIC GOALSCORER? During my school days scoring goals was never a problem and in my first season as an apprentice at Arsenal I hit 30 for the youth team. The following year I hit 59 for the youth and reserve teams.

WHO WERE YOUR GOALSCORING HEROES AS A YOUNGSTER? I supported Arsenal as a kid and my favourite player was always Charlie George – he was a real entertainer. I also enjoyed watching John Radford who scored some valuable goals for the club.

WAS IT ALWAYS YOUR AMBITION TO EMULATE THE LIKES OF GEORGE AND RADFORD AND BECOME A HIGHBURY HERO YOURSELF? I did have trials with a few other London clubs, including West Ham, Millwall and Chelsea, but as soon as Arsenal came in there was no decision to make. I went to the same school as Michael Thomas, who was also at Chelsea with me, and seeing him succeed at Highbury made me all the more determined to follow suit.

WHAT HAS BEEN THE HIGHLIGHT OF YOUR CAREER SO FAR? Making my debut as a substitute against Everton and scoring my first goal against Nottingham Forest are high on my list, but winning the FA Youth Cup a few years ago also meant a lot to me. I scored in every round and struck a hat-trick in the Final.

DID YOU WIN ANY ENGLAND HONOURS AT SCHOOLBOY OR YOUTH INTERNATIONAL LEVEL? No, although I did play in a trial match for the England youth side at one stage. I scored five goals in the game too and thought I was in with a shout of making the team but, for some reason, it didn't happen. I was disappointed at the time but it will all be forgotten if I make the Under-21 squad.

WHAT DOES YOUR FAMILY THINK OF YOUR RISE TO STARDOM? They are very proud of me – all 12 of them! Mum and Dad have always given me every encouragement and my five brothers and five sisters are right behind me. Mind you they keep my feet on the ground and there's no chance of me getting too big for my boots.

HOW VALUABLE WERE YOUR TWO LOAN SPELLS AT ORIENT AND LEICESTER? Playing first team football in the Fourth and Second Divisions provided me with vital experience and I considered both spells as important parts of my football education.

Lennie's lifeline rescued
WILLIAMS

"**I**F at first you don't succeed, try, try and try again," as the old saying goes. To which Charlton's England 'B' international Paul Williams might add: "And if you still don't succeed, keep trying until you do!"

Williams is a model of persistence. The small but swift striker suffered countless rejections from League clubs but never lost his self-belief and he was finally signed as a professional for Charlton Athletic at the age of 21.

The talented youngster from West Ham took the hard route to the top, via non-league football, while he sensibly trained for another career as a chartered accountant.

From the age of 17, Williams wrote to a host of clubs, and although Tottenham gave him a trial, the general response was poor, and he even stopped playing football for a year, such was the disappointment.

But at 18 he began to play semi-professional football for a local club, Clapton, moving from left-back to striker with great success. Fulham showed an interest in Williams and he started playing for their reserves.

Spotted

Sometimes he would play for Fulham on a Saturday morning and Clapton in the afternoon, but his devotion was not matched by Fulham's offer and he returned to the semi-pro ranks. He went from Clapton to Aveley and then on to Southern League Woodford Town, where he was spotted by Charlton manager Lennie Lawrence.

"I didn't realise he had been knocked back by so many clubs when I signed him," says Lawrence, who invested £10,000 for his signature. "Charlton gave him an 18-month contract and he probably realised it was his last opportunity to make the grade."

Williams a qualified accountant, still found life at Charlton "an uphill struggle". He admits: "I set myself a target of first-team football in two and a half months, but I didn't get a chance for one and a half years." Instead he was loaned to Third Division Brentford for a spell which saw him score seven goals in eight games. He played six times for the Charlton first-team in the 1987-88 season, without scoring, and he seemed to be going nowhere.

But when Charlton had three first choice strikers injured at the start of 1988-89, Williams seized his chance. He scored two goals in the 3-1 win over his boyhood heroes, West Ham, and followed up with another double strike as the League leaders Norwich went down by the same score.

Williams struck nine goals in 12 games by November, but then a torn cartilage put him out of action for six weeks, forcing him to miss a rare Charlton success, in the televised 'Soccer Six' tournament. But Williams was back for the New Year, and he carried on where he had left off – scoring goals.

By the end of his first full season Williams was the club's top scorer with 17 goals.

Although Charlton were sadly relegated last season, Paul continued to impress and established himself as one of the game's hottest properties.

WORTHY'S WINNERS

FRANK WORTHINGTON played in an era when goalscorers used to celebrate their success in style.

Worthy can still recall the trademarks of Britain's top marksman as they put their own personal signatures on the goals they scored.

Worthy recalls: "Kids in the parks used to copy every move in a striker's post-goal routine because each individual style was easily recognisable and regularly repeated.

"But where have all the unique celebrations gone these days? British players seem to have lost their flair for stamping their personal character and colour on a triumphant occasion.

"I don't believe strikers milk the fans' applause with the same flair as they used to and I can't say there are many characters in the game."

Worthy particularly recalls the scoring traits of the following famous five:

Allan Clarke (Leeds United) used to trot nonchalantly away from the goalmouth where he had just netted,

Denis Law — No.1

John Fashanu — aeroplane ace

John Barnes celebrates Law style

Lee Chapman — old hat

Charlie George — grounded

using those familiar short, tip-toe paces. He would always have one arm raised, his fist unclenched in a beautifully arrogant wave to the crowd.

Denis Law (Manchester United and Manchester City) used to walk away after scoring with a priceless, cheeky grin on his face. He differed from Clarke because he would clench his fist except for one significant finger pointing skywards. That showed where he lay in everyone's estimation … number one.

Mick Channon (Southampton and England) was famous for his "windmill" celebration, his arm whizzing round and round as he sprinted towards the touchline in triumph. I was never too keen on that myself but at least it was memorable.

Charlie George (Arsenal) used to lie on the ground after scoring with his arms outstretched and wait for his team-mates to dash up and lie on top of him. Eventually they would pick him up as he remained stiff as a board in the same emphatic position. That one trait made Arsenal's 1971 Cup Final victory over Liverpool unforgettable as George fired the

extra-time winner.

Peter Lorimer (Leeds) would raise both hands above his head and clap himself after scoring with his famous "seal" impersonation.

There were hundreds of other true characters with their own unique styles of celebration.

But apart from the following, Worthy reckons that celebrating in style these days has generally been left to the hip-swinging American Footballers.

John Fashanu (Wimbledon) does his famous "aeroplane" impersonation when he knocks one in for Wimbledon. The Dons are one of my least favourite teams but all credit to Fash for at least showing the personal touch. Arms are spread full length on either side in aero-dynamic magnificence as he leans first one way then the other in celebration.

John Barnes (Liverpool) trots away wagging a finger at the crowd to show the crowd, as Law used to, who is number one.

Lee Chapman sprints away with both arms outstretched above his head, fists unclenched, in perhaps the most

popular pose of all among players. But most of the celebrations these days don't deserve too many congratulations. They are mostly old hat and lacking that personal touch.

Hugo Sanchez (Real Madrid) is perhaps the greatest of all, specialising in an acrobatic somersault each time he hits the net for the Spanish giants or his native Mexico.

But perhaps the brilliant Sanchez illustrates my point … the true stylists and real entertainers aren't English these days.

It is a fun topic with a serious post-script. Crowds need entertainers. After all, that is what they pay to see. The more a player can develop that personal touch after scoring, the more he guarantees his own popularity with the fans.

And a cult figure is precisely what brings the border-line supporters out on to the terraces on a cold and rainy day.

If only the likes of Frank Worthington, Denis Law, Allan Clarke, Charlie George and Mick Channon were around today!

Worthy Fact-File

Born Halifax in November 1948. Joined Huddersfield as an apprentice in November 1966. Made 166 appearances and hit 42 goals before transferring to Leicester in August 1972. Made 209 appearances scoring 72 goals. Moved to Bolton in September 1977 (81 games — 35 goals). Joined Birmingham November 1979 (71 games — 30 goals).
Then played for Leeds (1981-82- 32 games — 14 goals).
Sunderland (1982 — 18 games — 2 goals).
Southampton (1983 — 34 games — 4 goals).
Brighton (1984 — 27 games — 7 goals).
Tranmere (1985-86 — 51 games — 21 goals.
Preston (1986-87 — 10 games — 3 goals).
Stockport (1987 — 18 games — 6 goals).
Frank also won 8 full England caps. He is now involved with former Chelsea, Arsenal, Stoke and England star Alan Hudson, coaching youngsters.

Hugo Sanchez — goals go to his head

TITLE DRIVES CLOUGHIE ON

The FA Cup is the one trophy to elude Brian Clough in his glittering career.

But aiming to win the coveted prize at Wembley was not the driving force behind him continuing the longest managerial career in English football with one club.

Clough, now 55 and in his 16th year at the City Ground, would dearly like to land the First Division title that he has captured for both Derby County and Nottingham Forest.

He admits: "I've been close to the FA Cup finals twice and on both occasions we were seen off by Liverpool amid major disappointment.

"It hurts when you get so near to a final and fail but all the time I have been in this business the one thing that has got me going more than anything else is the First Division title.

"It's the same when we start any season – if anyone asks me what prize I would like to win I would say the Championship before they had got the words out of their mouth.

"That's why finishing ninth last season disappointed me so much despite the fact that we went back to Wembley and won the Littlewoods Cup again.

"If we had finished in the bottom half of the table it would have absolutely creased me but at least we got our act together over the last couple of matches."

Cloughie and Peter Taylor receive the Championship trophy after Derby County's success in May 1972.

CASH IN ON BARGAIN BUYS

The success of bargain basement signings has been a key to Nottingham Forest's success in recent years. And nothing has changed.

Forest have made regular raids on the non-League market in particular and turned part-time players into First Division stars.

The likes of Garry Birtles, Peter Davenport, Steve Wigley and Gary Crosby have all made the grade in the First Division – and there's a promise that several other unknowns will soon follow them.

Forest have high hopes that midfield man Ian Woan, a £70,000 capture from the GM Vauxhall Conference side Runcorn, will prove to be a snip at the price.

Woan, who had been trailed by Merseyside pair Liverpool and Everton among others, was on the brink of signing for Bournemouth when Forest pounced at the eleventh hour to offer him the prospect of a First Division future at the City Ground.

And in the short time that he has been with Forest, he's made an impression on manager Brian Clough and the coaching staff.

Said Clough: "We like what we have seen of him so far. I take to anyone who can pass a ball properly – and that's a quality this lad has.

"He's got a very sweet left foot and although he's still got a lot to do, there's something for us to work on."

Woan himself has no doubts that he picked the right club in Forest. He revealed: "I felt sorry for Bournemouth because I was on the verge of signing for them but if you get a chance to join a top First Division club you have to take it."

Forest also have other non-League signings Stuart Cash, a left back from Halesowen, and former Leicester United pair Tony Loughlan and Neil Lyne aiming to get to the top.

Des Walker has matured into a player of true world class.

Ian Woan.

SHIPSTONES
Fine Beers

NEW DEAL FOR DES

The best bit of business Nottingham Forest conducted last season did not come in the shape of a new signing.

The day that Des Walker put his signature to a new contract at the club was undoubtedly the best deal that manager Brian Clough struck.

Having established himself as an England regular and continued to turn in the kind of performances that make him the country's outstanding defender, Walker could surely have taken his pick of top clubs at home and abroad had he wanted to move on.

But Walker explained: "I know a lot of people expected me to be looking for a transfer at the end of my contract at Forest — but why should I leave this club?

"I'm very content in Nottingham — I like the place, I like the club, I'm working with a great bunch of lads under the right kind of management.

"On top of that we've been to Wembley three times in just over 12 months and come back with three trophies. How many clubs can match that?

"Even last season when we didn't have as good a time as the previous year we were still good enough to retain the Littlewoods Cup and there's no reason why we can't carry on being as successful in coming years."

Forest fans have a favourite chant of "You'll never beat Des Walker." And first team coach Liam O'Kane enthuses: "He's such a good player that when he makes a mistake, you almost expect to hear about it on News at Ten!"

CELEBRITY

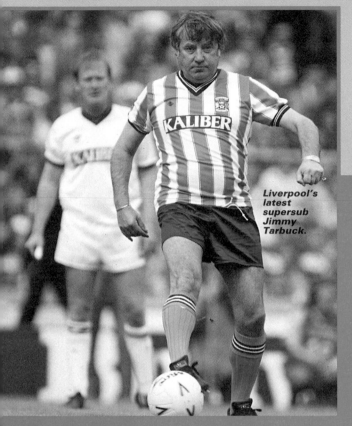

Liverpool's latest supersub Jimmy Tarbuck.

Nigel Benn shields the ball from Jasper Carrott and Paul Usher (Brookside's Barry Grant).

Steve Cram closes in on David Frost.

Frank Bruno and Daley Thompson take their football very seriously!

CITY F.C.

If you asked every schoolboy up and down the country what they would like to be when they leave school, the majority would probably reply ... a professional footballer.

And if you then asked many stars from the world of showbusiness and sport what they would love to do as an alternative career, soccer player would prove a very popular response.

Just look at some of the fit (or maybe not so fit), young (no comment!) stars SHOOT spotted indulging in their favourite pastime.

But don't think for a moment that they play simply for fun ... for most it's a deadly serious business once they walk out onto the hallowed turf.

Scotland's number one fan ... Rod Stewart.

Former Eastender Tom Watt has lofty ambitions to play for his beloved Arsenal.

TERRIBLE, traumatic, but finally ... tremendous. That was the 1989-90 season for Manchester United.

The Reds got off to a terrific start thrashing champions Arsenal 4-1 at Old Trafford in front of a 47,000 crowd entertained by the ball skills of the man they thought was destined to be chairman.

Michael Knighton was unknown in soccer circles on August 17, but two days later he was being hailed a hero by thousands of United followers.

As it turned out Mr Knighton's dream became a nightmare as the season progressed and eventually he pulled out of the takeover and became a director of the club.

Talk of the takeover was always in the background: "We talk about it in the dressing room, but I don't think it's had any effect on the way we play ... nor do I think that the club's name's been dragged down by all the publicity," said Bryan Robson mid-way through an injury-hit campaign which saw United fighting against relegation.

Older supporters were making comparisons with the team of 1963 which avoided the drop and went on to win the FA Cup. An omen, if ever there was one.

At that time United were blooding new players, and two seasons later the Law, Best and Charlton era saw two Championship wins as the Reds became England's first European Cup holders.

The team that took United into the new decade included expensive signings like Gary Pallister, Neil Webb, Paul Ince, Danny Wallace and Michael Phelan – £7 million worth of talent bought during a summer and early season spending spree by Alex Ferguson. Like their predecessors in the '60s they struggled to find cohesion.

It was a different story in the FA Cup though.

They took the difficult route, playing every round away from home, but they won their way through to an exciting Semi-Final against neighbours Oldham which was eventually decided by one of the young stars to emerge during the run.

Mark Robins grabbed the winner in a tense replay, knocking out his home town team. Robins is the son of an Oldham Police chief inspector, and almost needed Dad to escort him home after that!

United reached Wembley and the traumas of the season turned to torture for goalkeeper Jim Leighton.

He took the blame for slip-ups in a 3-3 draw against Steve Coppell's Crystal Palace and was sensationally dropped for the replay.

Lee Martin scores the FA Cup Final replay winner ... and relieves the pressure on his boss.

FERGIE

United boss saved by Cup triumph

United made a great start to the 1989-90 season ... thrashing the then Champions Arsenal 4-1 at Old Trafford. Brian McClair scores United's third.

In goal for the second game was Les Sealey who had taken over from an injured Leighton for games at QPR and against championship contenders Aston Villa during April.

Sealey was on loan from Luton and United won both games to stave off relegation, so Les was a hero before Wembley.

On the night of the replay he did it again, holding out against a Palace side which tried to take the physical route to success, and nobody celebrated more than Les when former YTS boy Lee Martin raced 70 yards to get onto the end of a Neil Webb pass and score the winner.

"This is the greatest moment of my career," Alex Ferguson announced. "But leaving out Jim Leighton was the worst. It was a decision I had to make. We have won the FA Cup, now let's see if we can go further."

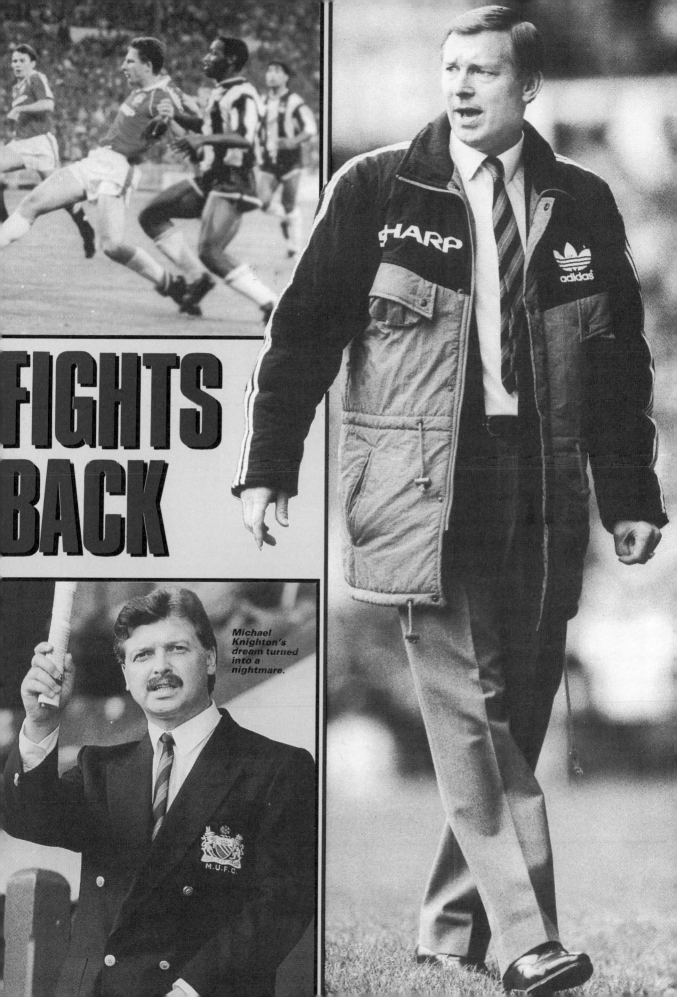

FIGHTS BACK

Michael Knighton's dream turned into a nightmare.

SQUARED-UP

The SHOOT photographer has obviously been working without his glasses again. So, use the clues to discover the identity of our six scrambled stars.

ANSWERS BELOW

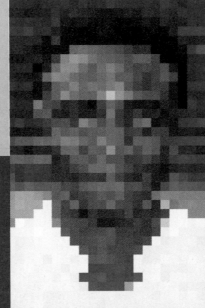

1. Not the true Blue striker, but a First Division defender who goes gunning for forwards.

2. Howe's that ... a real tiny terror whose fine form last season earned him a place in the England team.

3. A losing Wembley skipper, but his club won fame for their royal performance.

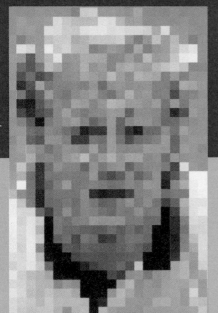

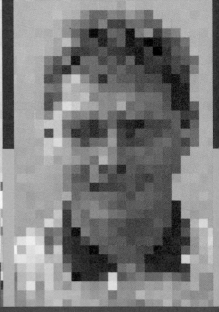

4. Proved the right man for England after a late injury scare almost put him out of the World Cup.

5. Found fame in the Scottish Premier. A real stylish midfielder now worth a fortune.

6. On the main road to success this young captain is a real inspiration especially when he sees red.

MAURICE MALPASS

DUNDEE UNITED

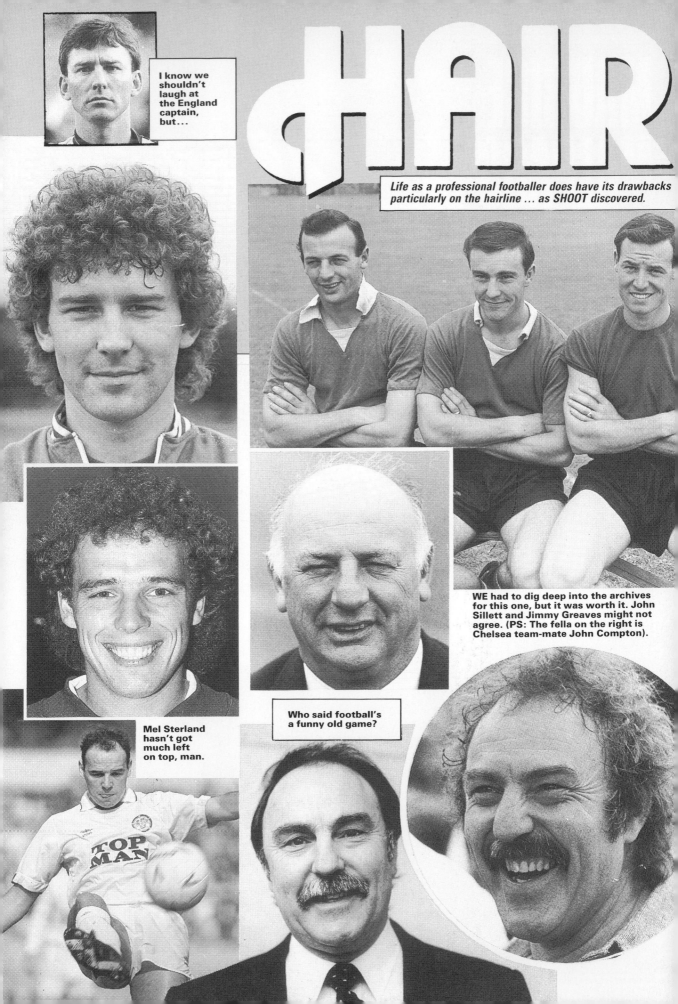

I know we shouldn't laugh at the England captain, but...

HAIR

Life as a professional footballer does have its drawbacks particularly on the hairline ... as SHOOT discovered.

WE had to dig deep into the archives for this one, but it was worth it. John Sillett and Jimmy Greaves might not agree. (PS: The fella on the right is Chelsea team-mate John Compton).

Mel Sterland hasn't got much left on top, man.

Who said football's a funny old game?

TODAY, GONE TOMORROW

..but what the hell happened to Walshy?

Paul Walsh always did like to be different.

Conclusive proof that Ray Wilkins DID have hair ... once upon a long time ago.

Don't worry. Bobby Gould got his money back from Grecian 2000.

GIANT X WORD

Clues Across

1 Rising star at Highbury (8)
4 Forfar Athletic reside here (7,4)
11 Word which prefixes 'side' and 'target' (2)
12 Number favoured by Paul Gascoigne at Spurs (5)
13 Mirren or Etienne (2)
14 Republic of Ireland star from Anfield (6)
16 One of soccer's governing bodies (1,1)
17 Lofthouse, perhaps (3)
18 He's the king at the Baseball Ground (6)
19 How many times Coventry have won the FA Cup (3)
20 Oldham's Hallworth (3)
21 'Big ...' – nickname of famous English boss (3)
22 To leave out of the side (4)
23 Superstitious footballers might believe in one (4)
25 How many goals Liverpool thumped past Crystal Palace in a single game last season (4)
26 Brian to Nigel (3)

29 Castle or Port, perhaps (3)
33 Go down this lane and you'll find Bury FC (4)
34 City where Norway play most of their home games (4)
35 What players might do after a goal (3)
36 Hartford, the former Scottish international (3)
37 ...ll – Christian name of Eire striker (3)
38 Animal found grazing in Derby, perhaps (3,3)
39 John Barnes scored a memorable goal here (3)
41 Tissier or Havre (2)
42 Can be found on a shirt (6)
43 He wears the number one, initially (1,1)
45 Young Villa striker came good last season (5)
46 .. Ahead Eagles – unusually named club from Holland (2)
48 These can cost a club dearly (8,3)
49 Relative Brian Clough calls 'Jackie Cougan' (8)

Clues Down

1 Home of the Canaries (6,4)
2 Winger who was described as the 'Scottish George Best' when he came down to England in the 70s (9)
3 Second Division Champions or road in Huddersfield (5)
5 Manager of 13 down (6)
6 ...ttenham (2)
7 A poor performance, perhaps (5)
8 He's played in two FA Cup finals for two different London clubs (4,5)
9 Vauxhall Conference club who once boasted both Robbie Cooke and Ernie Moss (9)
10 Hit man for the Blades (5)
13 Scottish First Division Champions last season (2,9)
15 City which provided a home for the First Division Championship trophy in 1978 (10)
16 The Saddlers play here (7,4)
18 Young Celtic full-back (5,5)
24 Manchester United chairman,

initially (1,1)
27 A quality all players should possess (10)
28 Member of the Royal family, presented the FA Cup to Dave Beasant in 1988 (2)
30 Twice winner of the Football Writers Player of the Year award (4,6)
31 West Brom midfielder with a famous brother (4,6)
32 They are sometimes called this at Boothferry Park (3,6)
40 Wimbledon's FA Cup triumph, for example (3,3)
41 Millwall are also known as these (5)
43 Aberdeen's young Watson (5)
44 Road which takes you to the home of last season's 92nd placed club (5)
47 Orient's nickname (2)

ANSWERS ON PAGE 121

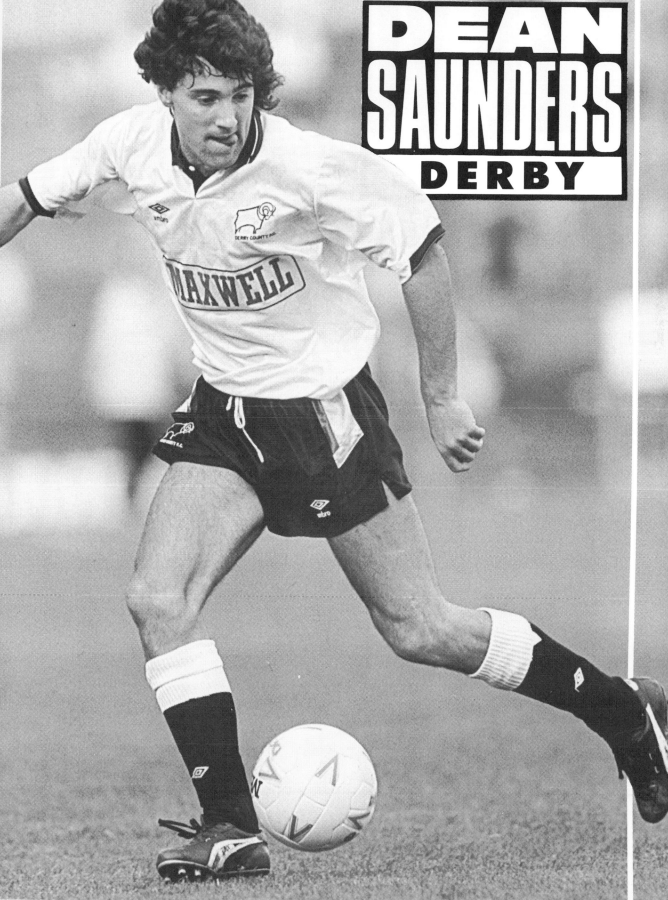
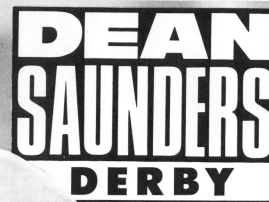

DEAN SAUNDERS
DERBY

THE YORKSHIRE

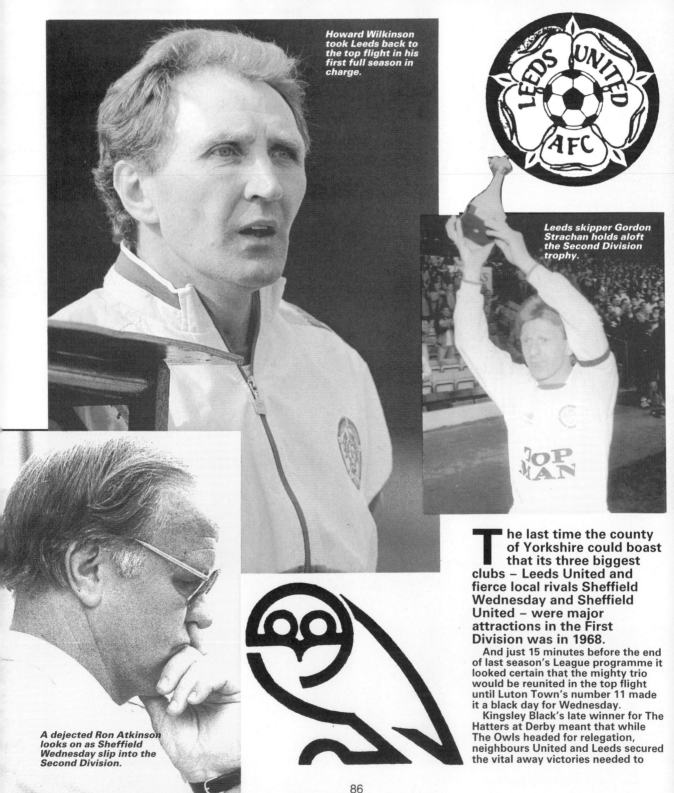

Howard Wilkinson took Leeds back to the top flight in his first full season in charge.

Leeds skipper Gordon Strachan holds aloft the Second Division trophy.

A dejected Ron Atkinson looks on as Sheffield Wednesday slip into the Second Division.

The last time the county of Yorkshire could boast that its three biggest clubs – Leeds United and fierce local rivals Sheffield Wednesday and Sheffield United – were major attractions in the First Division was in 1968.

And just 15 minutes before the end of last season's League programme it looked certain that the mighty trio would be reunited in the top flight until Luton Town's number 11 made it a black day for Wednesday.

Kingsley Black's late winner for The Hatters at Derby meant that while The Owls headed for relegation, neighbours United and Leeds secured the vital away victories needed to

CAVALRY

Blades boss Dave Bassett celebrates promotion with wife Christine.

Sheffield United's dynamic duo Brian Deane and Tony Agana.

United's defence couldn't prevent Leeds winning 4-0 at Elland Road.

take them in the opposite direction.

Although it's true to say that the whole of Sheffield was eagerly looking forward to two sell-out steel city derby games, the Leeds v United matches generated a fair bit of interest themselves last season.

A sell-out crowd of 31,602 witnessed the 2-2 draw on Boxing Day at Bramall Lane while 32,727 were packed in to Elland Road as Leeds demolished The Blades 4-0 to virtually seal the Second Division Championship.

Now Yorkshire's sleeping giants, driven forward by the hugely popular managers Dave Bassett and Howard Wilkinson, aim to rival the achievements of the neighbouring county of Lancashire by winning some silverware.

CLUES ACROSS

1 Sounds like buyers are needed North of the border for a Blackburn player (5-7)
7 Obviously not the ground where Plymouth Argyle play away (4-4)
8 (See 21 across)
9 Jimmy ————, former Man. United defender who has had two spells with Rangers (7)
10 Chelsea player of the past taken from a schoolboy league? (5)
13 ———— Finney, famous player of the past (3)
15 Terrible news to a Bristol Rovers defender (anag) (6)
17+22A Watford striker, ex Wimbledon and Newcastle Utd (4-6)
20 Tony ————, Sheffield United striker (5)
21+8A Or let beer spill over a Charlton player (anag) (6-3)
22 (See 17 across)

CLUES DOWN

1 European Cup winners in 1983 (2-7)
2 Brendan ————, Leeds United defender (6)
3 Kenny ————, ex-Chelsea and Villa stalwart, now with Crewe (5)
4 The luck I change for an Arsenal player (anag) (5)
5 Shaun ————, Sunderland midfielder for 10 years, now with Blackpool (7)
6 Jim ————, Tranmere striker, previously Oldham, Port Vale and Wrexham (5)
11 Old news spread about a Barnsley player (anag) (7)
12 Forename of the Man City manager (6)
14 Steve ————, Reading striker previously with Leicester and Reading (5)
16 Alan ————, for three years he was strike partner with Gary Lineker at Leicester (5)
18 Venue in Mexico for England's defeat by West Germany in 1970 World Cup (4)
19 A very windy experience for the whole country, though West Ham have their very own (4)

Compiled by Trevor Hungerford

ANSWERS ON PAGE 121

Did you Know?..

STRANRAER OF THE SCOTTISH LEAGUE DIVISION TWO, WERE THE *LAST* SCOTTISH LEAGUE CLUB TO INSTALL *FLOODLIGHTS* BACK IN JUNE 1981.

WHY DON'T WE GET FLOODLIGHTS JIMMY?
CAN'T SEE NOTHING!
HATE THESE DARK NIGHTS!
OCH AYE!
SHAN'T COME AGAIN!

LEARN THE RAY ROYCE WAY

I hate summer training. These beach balls are too light.

CLOUGHIE QUOTES

'I want to be manager of Scotland' ... Cloughie in 1985.
'It's easy enough to get to Ireland. Just walk straight across the Irish Sea'
... Cloughie, on his application to become manager of the Republic of Ireland a few months later.
'I can't promise to give a team talk in Welsh, but from now on I shall be taking my holidays in Porthcawl and I've bought a complete set of Harry Secombe albums'
... Cloughie on hopes of being appointed manager of Wales in 1988.
'I'm a bighead, not a figurehead'
... Cloughie on why he has refused several company directorships.

FORMING A WALL IS EXTREMELY IMPORTANT! A GOOD WALL CAN PREVENT GOALS FROM FREE-KICKS!

BOOT! WHACK!

SEE-Sob!-WHAT I MEAN?

SPOT THE DIFFERENCE

Our artist has made six changes to the cartoon in B. Can you spot them?

A

B

Memorable Moments In Football ...

BIG GAMES ARE STAGED OUTSIDE LONDON FOR A CHANGE

ST JAMES' PARK

AWAY ME BONNEY ENGLAND BOUS!

HUSBAND/WILKIE

SNAP SHOTS

Mo Johnston makes a point where he'd like the next corner-kick to head for.

Bruce Grobbelaar's way of telling the Kop that the ball just missed his goal by a mile.

Oi what's the name of the sheep who plays 1st DIVISION Soccer?

Mark Ewes... Ha Ha... He's always hitting the Baa. Ha Ha get it?

Pooh

Notta lotta people

KISSING BULL

England striker Steve Bull has an unusual superstition – before every Wolves game he kisses his No.9 shirt three times. Before he came into professional football with W.B.A., he worked 12 hours a day in a builder's yard, and spent much of the time humping bags of cement. "That's where I get my strength from," says Bull, who has been Wolves' top scorer for the past three seasons.

Thorvaldur Orlygsson, Nottingham Forest's Icelandic international forward, interrupted law studies back home to come into big-time football here. He's known in the Forest dressing-room as "Toddy."

If Charlton's dream of moving back to The Valley comes true, one of their players will certainly feel at home. Robert Lee used to work a turnstile there before he joined the club's playing staff.

On Boxing Day 1962, Sunderland centre-forward Brian Clough sustained a knee injury that ended his playing career. On Boxing Day 1984, son Nigel made his League debut for manager Brian's club Nottingham Forest.

PC OGGY

For two years before Coventry City goalkeeper Steve Ogrizovic made a career in football (previous clubs Chesterfield, Liverpool and Shrewsbury), he was a police constable in Nottingham . . . shared a beat with ice skating super-star-to-be Christopher Dean.

England captain Bryan Robson left school without any "O" levels. Explanation: He was "too interested" in football!

Six Time Loser

Huddersfield Town are the only club in Football League history to score six goals in a match and finish up losers. It happened in a Second Division match at Charlton on December 21, 1957. With 20 minutes left, Huddersfield led 5-1, and injury had reduced Charlton to ten men. But the result was Charlton 7, Huddersfield 6.

FIRST RESULTS

Have you ever wondered what the classified results were on the day the Football League began? It was September 8, 1888, and this is how the games finished:

Bolton Wanderers 3 Derby County 6
Everton 2 Accrington 1
Preston North End 5 Burnley 2
Stoke 0 West Bromwich Albion 2
Wolverhampton W 1 Aston Villa 1

The other two clubs, Blackburn Rovers and Notts County, kicked off a week later.

Cup-winner Gazza

Paul Gascoigne, hoping to win a major prize with Tottenham, already has a Cup medal. He captained Newcastle United when they won the F.A. Youth Cup in 1985.

Houdini Blues

After Arsenal, Everton and Liverpool, the club with the longest current membership of the First Division are Coventry City, who have played in the Championship since 1967. During this time, they have survived no fewer than NINE relegation battles.

Nigel Howard Clough in action

Steve Bull

know that....

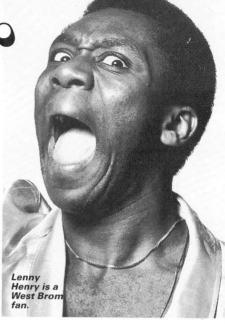

Lenny Henry is a West Brom fan.

What's in a name?

What's your middle name? Here are some belonging to top people in football: Kerry MICHAEL Dixon . . . Alvin EDWARD Martin . . . Kenneth MATHIESON Dalglish . . . David ANTHONY O'Leary . . . Graeme JAMES Souness . . . Stephen ROGER Bruce . . . Christopher ROLAND Waddle . . . David ROBERT Speedie . . . Neil JOHN Webb . . . Terry IAN Butcher . . . Peter LESLIE Shilton . . . Trevor McGREGOR Steven . . . Frank ALEXANDER Carr . . . Brian HOWARD Clough . . . Nigel HOWARD Clough . . . Gary WINSTON Lineker.

Could a non-League club win the F.A. Cup this season? You have to go back to the start of the century to find the last time it happened – Tottenham Hotspur as a Southern League club in 1901.

Nicknames

John Barnes is known as "Digger," . . . Manchester United striker Mark Hughes is "Sparky" . . . and Chelsea manager Bobby Campbell calls left-back Graeme Le Saux "Le Socks."

Famous fans: Tim Brooke-Taylor (Derby County), Graham Gooch (West Ham, Willie Thorne (Gary Lineker), Steve Cram (Sunderland), Rodney Bewes (Chelsea), Lenny Henry (W.B.A.), Bernard Manning (Manchester City), Rod Stewart (Scotland), Eric Sykes (Oldham Athletic), Bobby Davro (Tottenham), Roy Hudd (Crystal Palace), Desmond Lynam (Brighton).

Graeme Le Saux

Snooker star Willie Thorne is a great fan of Gary Lineker

OLDHAM'S BRAVE BATTLE

THE NEARLY MEN

BEFORE the 1989-90 season started Oldham Athletic had not won a single major honour in their 95-year history, unless of course you count the Division Three North Championship in 1952-53 and the Third Division title in 1973-74.

By the end of last season The Latics hadn't won a trophy of any great significance. But, boy … did they come close.

Joe Royle's never-say-die battlers played 65 games in all competitions, but came away with nothing except fond memories of reaching the Littlewoods Cup Final and two epic FA Cup Semi-Final meetings with Manchester United.

But perhaps the greatest disappointment of all was to miss out on promotion to the First Division. In the end, tiredness and mounting injury problems took their toll on Royle's squad as they finished eighth, narrowly missing out on a play-off spot.

This season The Latics aim to fulfil their ambition of returning to the top flight after an absence of 68 years.

Frank Bunn's record-breaking sixth goal in Oldham's Littlewoods Cup-tie v Scarborough.

Earl Barrett scores Oldham's third goal in their 6-0 thrashing of West Ham in the Littlewoods Cup. Opponents feared the power of Andy Ritchie (below).

Earl Barrett was again on target in the thrilling 3-3 FA Cup Semi-Final draw v Manchester United.

Proud in defeat ... although Oldham lost 1-0 to Nottingham Forest at Wembley they won the hearts of millions with their performance.

OI REF!

Here we capture some of our top referees in lighter moments. Turn to pages 110-111 for a more serious look at life in the middle.

Keith Hackett finds the time to practice break-dancing during the Forest v Arsenal game.

Ray Lewis explains to Kettering 'keeper Kevin Shoemake why he disallowed a Northampton goal.

Roger Milford makes it quite clear to QPR's Simon Barker where he'll end up if the arguing persists.

John Martin asks Manchester City 'keeper Andy Dibble if he can have the ball back.

BORO'S BOLD REARGUARD ACTION

Skipper Tony Mowbray may have to fight for his place this season.

Middlesbrough skipper Tony Mowbray firmly believes the emergence of promising youngsters bodes well for the Ayresome club in the 1990s – and puts pressure on the senior players.

"The older men will be looking over their shoulders as the less experienced players challenge for their places," says Mowbray. "There is no chance of any complacency creeping in, which can sometimes happen to those who are used to regular selection."

Mowbray is confident that, in defence, Boro are well equipped to hold their own over the next ten years, due to the young talent that emerged as they fought to retain their Division Two status. Tony, as the senior member of his team's back four, is well qualified to air his views.

"I'm full of admiration for the way in which Simon Coleman, Nicky Mohan and Owen McGhee developed last

Owen McGhee

Simon Coleman.

Nicky Mohan

season," he says. "They made outstanding progress.

"When Gary Pallister left for Manchester United, Simon Coleman had the difficult job of taking his place, and to his credit he made the fans forget Pallister.

"And the £400,000 paid out for Simon, last September, will go down as one of the best investments of the season.

"When you consider that success at most clubs stems from a sound defence it's easy to see why I'm optimistic about Boro's future."

KEVIN BROCK

NEWCASTLE

SHOCKS of

1980

Halifax 1
Manchester City 0

FA Cup 3rd Round
Saturday January 5

HALIFAX: Kilner, Dunleavy, Hutt, Evans, Harris, Hendrie, Firth, Kennedy, Mountfield, Smith, Stafford.
MAN CITY: Corrigan, Ranson, Power, Reid, Caton, Bennett, Henry, Daley, Robinson, Viljoen, Shinton.

ALLISON BLUNDERLAND

CITY'S flamboyant boss Malcolm Allison was again the victim of a hypnotist's curse as his £3million misfits were sent spinning out of the cup by two-bob Town.

Allison, who was supposed to be celebrating his first anniversary as coaching supremo at Maine Road, had been haunted by the infamous showbiz freak Romark since his days as manager of Crystal Palace.

Romark, real name Robert Markham, claimed to have cast a spell on Allison and his teams after an offer to help Palace in 1976 was turned down.

The curse struck again at The Shay where Romark had spent several hours working on the Halifax players, turning the Fourth Division no-hopers into world beaters.

Midfielder Paul Hendrie was the hero of the hour, scoring the only goal of the game, but Halifax boss George Kirby insisted: "Romark made all the difference. He made everyone feel we couldn't possibly lose."

Dejected City striker Michael Robinson wasn't so complimentary, however. "Romark wants stuffing," he moaned.

1981

Exeter 4
Newcastle 0

FA Cup 5th Round Replay
Wednesday, February 18

EXETER: Bond, Rogers M, Sparrow, Forbes, Roberts L, Roberts P, Pearson, Rogers P, Kellow, Delve, Hatch.
NEWCASTLE: Carr, Carney, Johnson, Shoulder, Boam, Halliday, Walker, Trewick, Clarke, Wharton, Waddle.

HAIL THE CORNFLAKE KID

PETER Hatch, 'The Cornflake Kid', poured cold milk on any ideas Newcastle had of going all the way to Wembley.

After holding their more illustrious

1981 ... Exeter celebrate knocking mighty Newcastle out of the FA Cup.

rivals to a 1-1 draw in the first match, the cream of Devon licked United in a remarkable replay – with Hatch leading the charge.

Peter the Great, whose pre-match meal was two bowls of Kellogs cornflakes, made sure that the Grecians didn't make a meal of their task by putting his side ahead after just 13 minutes.

It certainly wasn't a case of unlucky 13 for Exeter who went onto record an emphatic victory – and so march into the FA Cup Quarter Finals for the first time in 50 years!

Ian Pearson added a second after 19 minutes and Peter Rogers made it 3-0 just before the half-time break. His cousin Martin completed the rout in the closing stages.

Afterwards, jubilant Exeter boss Brian Godfrey, whose side had already dumped Leicester and Millwall out of the competition, beamed: "We've seen off the Lions (Millwall), The Magpies (Newcastle), now for the Cockerels."

His reference was to Tottenham who Exeter met in the next round, but sadly the giant-killing ended at White Hart Lane where Spurs won 2-0.

1982

Chelsea 2
Liverpool 0

FA Cup 5th Round
Saturday February 13

CHELSEA: Francis, Locke, Hutchings, Nutton, Droy, Pates, Rhoades-Brown, Hales, Lee C, Walker, Fillery.
LIVERPOOL: Grobbelaar, Neal, Lawrenson, Kennedy A, Whelan, Hansen, Dalglish, Lee S, Rush, McDermott, Souness.

RHOADESY-LEE BURY REDS

PETER Rhoades-Brown and Colin Lee combined to sink the Reds and put the Blues in the frame for a Wembley

visit.

Second Division Chelsea were given no chance of turning the tables of odds-on favourites Liverpool, despite being cheered on by a 41,000 crowd.

Those Stamford Bridge cheers turned to roars of delight as Rhoadsy and Lee left Bruce Grobbelaar grasping at thin air with the most precious goals of their career.

1983

Liverpool 1
Brighton 2

FA Cup 5th Round
Sunday February 20

LIVERPOOL: Grobbelaar, Neal, Kennedy, Lawrenson, Whelan, Hansen, Dalglish, Lee, Rush, Hodgson, Souness.
BRIGHTON: Digweed, Ramsey, Gatting, Grealish, Foster, Stevens, Case, Ward, Robinson, Ryan, Smillie.

CASE SERA SERA

FORMER Anfield hero Jimmy Case left

Hundreds of Chelsea fans scaled a cemetery wall and crossed railway lines to gain free entry into the ground and thousands more invaded the pitch in celebration after Lee's goals.

There were no celebrations in the Liverpool dressing room from which manager Bob Paisley emerged to say: "They caught us daydreaming. You can't play cocky boot stuff all the time."

1982 ... Peter Rhoades-Brown scores Chelsea's first goal against Liverpool.

the scene of some of his greatest triumphs with Liverpool fans shaking their fists at him in anger.

Jovial Jim was in party mood after scoring the winner as Brighton caused one of the upsets of the season.

Irishman Gerry Ryan had put the Seagulls on cloud nine after 32 minutes but it was left to Case to pull the master stroke a minute after Craig Johnston's equaliser.

Case was joined in the Brighton celebrations by one other Liverpudlian. Manager Jimmy Melia also played for the Reds and this was his greatest triumph as a manager.

Brighton went all the way to the final, only to lose to Manchester United in a replay, and were relegated the same season while Liverpool found solace in another Championship triumph.

Continued over the page

1984

Bournemouth 2
Manchester Utd 0

**FA Cup 3rd Round
Saturday January 7**

BOURNEMOUTH: Leigh, La Ronde, Sulley, Savage, Brown, Brignull, Train, Nightingale, Morgan, Graham M, Thompson.
MAN UTD: Bailey, Moses, Albiston, Wilkins, Hogg, Duxbury, Robson, Muhren, Stapleton, Whiteside, Graham A.

1984 ... Milton Graham (dark strip, on floor) scores one of the goals that shock Manchester United.

UNITED THEY FALL

RON Atkinson threatened to throw himself off the Bournemouth cliffs after Manchester United's second Cup humiliation in the space of 19 days.

United were still reeling from the Milk Cup defeat by Oxford and Big Ron confessed: "I feel ashamed. We let ourselves and our fans down badly. It is my worst hour in the game."

Atkinson said his Cup holders had 'failed to produce our class' but Bournemouth skipper was even more cutting when he said of United: "They had too many prima donnas. They are not in the same League as Liverpool."

Goals by Milton Graham and Ian Thompson within the space of two minutes in the second half set up manager Harry Redknapp's 'greatest day'.

Houchen ensured another day of FA Cup shame for the ghastly Gunners.

Arsenal had been knocked out in the early stages by lowly opposition no fewer than six times in the previous 52 years and little York delivered a sickening seventh blow.

It took a penalty in the dying seconds from Houchen to give City the victory they deserved and the goal hero gloated afterwards: "Arsenal didn't compete – that's why they are out."

In the Fifth Round York worked wonders to hold Liverpool to a 1-1 draw at Bootham Crescent, but they were no match in the replay at Anfield where they were crushed 7-0.

became the first non-League club to win an FA Cup tie to beat a Division One side on their own ground since the war.

The part-timers from the Gola League left the Blues battered and bewildered... particularly Robert Hopkins.

The fiery winger had put Birmingham ahead and seemingly on the road to victory after 64 minutes, only to see his effort cancelled out two minutes later by Ron Ellis.

Then, with just 16 minutes left on the clock, Hopkins the hero turned Hopkins the villain with a disastrous own goal which sent his club crashing out of the FA Cup.

Altrincham keeper Jeff Wealands, a former Birmingham player, said: "I fancied our chances from the moment the draw was made and I don't think anyone can say we didn't deserve to win."

1985

York 1
Arsenal 0

**FA Cup 4th Round
Saturday January 26**

YORK: Astbury, Senior, Hay, Sbraqia, MacPhail, Haslegrove, Ford, Butler, Walwyn, Houchen, Pearce.
ARSENAL: Lukic, Anderson, Sansom, Talbot, O'Leary, Caton, Robson, Williams, Mariner, Woodcock, Nicholas.

HOUCH! Pain for Arsenal

A LAST minute penalty by striker Keith

1986

Birmingham 1
Altrincham 2

**FA Cup 3rd Round
Tuesday January 14**

BIRMINGHAM: Seaman, Ranson, Dicks, Hagan, Armstrong, Kuhl, Bremner, Roberts, Kennedy, Platnauer, Hopkins.
ALTRINCHAM: Wealands, Gardner, Densmore, Johnson, Cuddy, Conning, Ellis, Davison, Reid, Chesters, Anderson.

BRUM HUMBLED

RENOWNED Cup fighters Altrincham

the EIGHTIES

1987

Aldershot 3
Oxford 0

FA Cup 3rd Round
Saturday January 10

ALDERSHOT: Lange, Blankley, Friar, Burvill, Smith, Wignall, Barnes, Mazzon, Ring, McDonald I, Langley.
OXFORD: Hardwick, Langan, McDonald R, Reck, Hebberd, Dreyer, Houghton, Aldridge, Whitehurst, Trewick, Brock.

BLOW FOR ALDO

JOHN Aldridge experienced the highs and lows of football within the space of a few days as Oxford were sent tumbling by Fourth Division Aldershot.

The week had begun in sensational fashion for Aldo who agreed a dream move to his home-town club Liverpool before returning to Oxford to boost their FA Cup hopes.

But there was to be no fairy tale ending to his Oxford career as Aldershot turned on the style to record one of the shocks of the season.

And it was a personal triumph for Colin Smith who had battled to overcome Hodgkinsons Disease, a cancer of the lymph glands, to guide his side to a famous victory.

Smith put the Shots ahead after just six minutes and Glenn Burvill and Bobby Barnes completed Oxford's misery in a second half rout.

It was just a shame that only 1,966 fans were there to witness a memorable performance, thousands boycotting the tie because ticket prices had been pumped up to £9 and £11 – the most expensive in cup history.

1988

Port Vale 2
Tottenham 1

FA Cup 4th Round
Saturday January 30

PORT VALE: Grew, Steggles, Hughes, Walker, Hazell, Sproson, Ford, Earle, Riley, Beckford, Cole.
TOTTENHAM: Parks, Hughton, Thomas, Ruddock, Fairclough, Mabbutt, Allen C, Allen P, Waddle, Fenwick, Moran.

WALKER'S CRISP STRIKE

A STUNNING goal by Ray Walker after just 12 minutes set Port Vale on the road to a famous victory over the aristocrats from White Hart Lane.

And when veteran defender Phil Sproson added a second 12 minutes later Tottenham were on the ropes in a one-sided fight which, had it been a boxing match, would have been stopped there and then.

Spurs succeeded in pulling a goal back through Neil Ruddock, but there was no denying Port Vale their well-deserved moment of triumph.

Hero Sproson was cutting in his criticism of the 'fancy dans' from North London.

"I was shocked at their attitude for such an important game. They didn't want to know. Their attitude was all wrong."

1987 ... First Division Oxford were shot down by Aldershot.

1988 ... Champagne shower for Port Vale boss John Rudge after beating Spurs.

1989

Sutton United 2
Coventry 1

FA Cup 3rd Round
Saturday January 7

SUTTON: Roffey, Jones, Rains, Golley, Pratt, Rogers, Stephens, Dawson, Dennis, McKinnon, Hanlan.
COVENTRY: Ogrizovic, Borrows, Phillips, Sedgley, Kilcline, Peake, Bennett, Speedie, Regis, McGrath, Smith.

MATT FINISH!

BRICKLAYER Matt Hanlan struck a sensational 60th minute winner to leave 1987 FA Cup winners Coventry mortar-fied.

It was one of the most remarkable acts of giant-killing the competition has known – and John Sillett's men could have few complaints.

After riding the early storm, when Coventry briefly threatened to blow the Vauxhall Conference club away, Sutton fought back with a vengeance and Tony Rains gave them a welcome lead just before the interval.

David Phillips levelled for City after 52 minutes but master brickie Hanlan pounced on the hour to cement a place in the soccer history books for the non-League club.

Manager Barrie Williams was still in dreamland when he said: "The enormity of this victory will take time to sink in. It is all so unreal."

GAME FOR A LAUGH

"Funny thing, boss. When I shoot with my left foot, my right sock falls down ... and when I shoot with my right the left falls down"

"Excuse me, ref, I would like to make a teeny, weeny protest"

"That's our new 'keeper. They call him The Cat"

"It's the ball you're supposed to put in the back of the net"

"There's a right potty nurse on the ward ... she supports Everton"

"Our new super striker spends 25 quid a week on his hair do"

"So, she's a member of our supporter's club is she? How interesting"

"But you've got to patch him up by Saturday, Doc, we're playing in the Cup"

"Of course there's only one shower. Have you seen them play lately?"

TIM BREAKER
LUTON

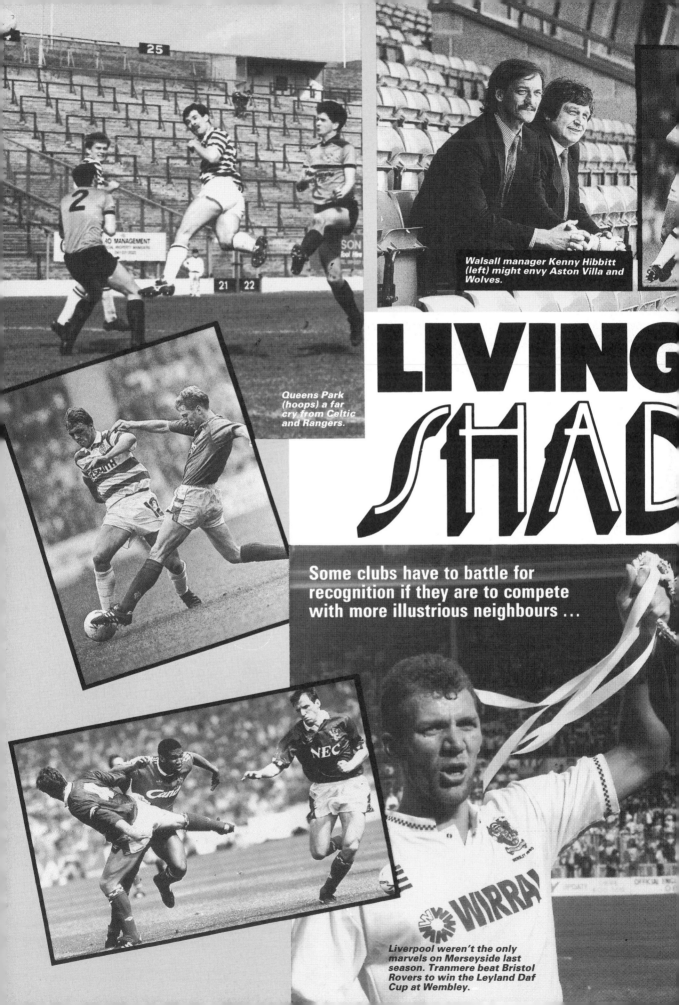

Walsall manager Kenny Hibbitt (left) might envy Aston Villa and Wolves.

LIVING SHAD

Queens Park (hoops) a far cry from Celtic and Rangers.

Some clubs have to battle for recognition if they are to compete with more illustrious neighbours …

Liverpool weren't the only marvels on Merseyside last season. Tranmere beat Bristol Rovers to win the Leyland Daf Cup at Wembley.

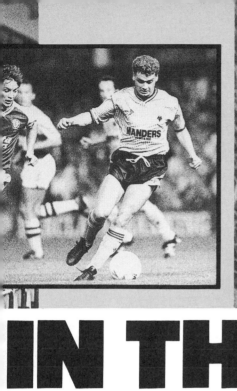

IN THE OWS

Back in the League
Darlington (white) don't
worry about Newcastle and
Sunderland.

Orient boss Frank
Clark would welcome
West Ham fans.

A Day in the Life of a Ref...

We've had our fun, now SHOOT takes a serious look at the job of a top referee. Without them the game couldn't be played. Yet they have a thankless task.

Brian Hill, a member of FIFA's referee's panel, gives his account of a typical matchday routine.

The game he chose was last season's First Division derby between Arsenal and Millwall.

Local derbies are always a bit special and I was quite excited about the prospect.

The night before the game I check my kit and make sure everything is there. I never leave anything to chance. I will go to bed fairly early on the Friday night because I like to have a good night's sleep. That helps set me up for the day ahead.

My wife prepares my kit for me and I'm very lucky because my family have always supported me and that's very important when things have not gone so well during a game.

HERE IS A RUN-DOWN OF MY TYPICAL PRE-MATCH DIARY

SATURDAY, APRIL 28: ARSENAL v MILLWALL

8.00am: I'm up bright and early and looking forward to the match. I do have a good English breakfast and that usually sees me through the day.

9.30am: I'm ready to leave home. Quite often one of the children will come and we leave Kettering and drive to Wellingborough to pick up my dad.

He always comes and is good company. He doesn't necessarily say much but it's nice to have him there just in case something goes wrong.

I like to leave myself plenty of time because it is not best to take chances when travelling on the M1. Arsenal is fairly easy to get to, it's 87 miles from Kettering to Highbury door to door, but I like to be at the ground nice and early.

12 Noon: I always aim to be at the ground by this time, three hours before kick-off. That might seem a little strange to be there so early but after driving for two-and-a-half hours I need to stretch my legs, relax and maybe soak up the atmosphere.

There was a lovely atmosphere building up and the crowd was starting to gather. I had a wander around the ground and went out to have a look at the pitch and have a chat with the groundsman. Even though we had had no rain for a while, the pitch looked in immaculate condition.

12.30pm: A cup of tea and a sit down for ten minutes. By 12.45pm the linesmen Mervyn Walker from Bury St Edmunds and Paul Hardy of Aylesbury had arrived. Two men I know quite well.

It's nice when I know the linesmen because I have to work closely with them on the

Rival managers on the day were George Graham (left) and Bruce Rioch.

pitch. Football is about three teams. We had Arsenal in red, Millwall in yellow and the three of us in black. People often forget about us.

We all took our guests upstairs and had a look at the Arsenal trophy room. That is another advantage of arriving early, it gives us a chance to see behind the scenes and show our guests around, which makes them feel part of it all.

1.30pm: We left our guests and went for another walk on the pitch and checked to make sure the nets were in good condition.

There was a marching band on the pitch entertaining the crowd and this is something we could perhaps do with more often. People want supporters in the ground earlier to avoid delayed kick-offs so why not give them something to watch?

2.00pm: We are back in the dressing room and beginning to sort out our kit. At most matches there is an assessor who watches our performance and he will come into the changing room and listen to what I say to my linesmen.

At this point the Police Inspector in charge of crowd control will come in and tell us what will happen in case of an emergency.

2.15pm: The two captains and the two managers (George Graham and newly appointed Bruce Rioch) come into our dressing room and they hand me their team-sheets. On the

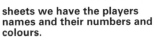

Arsenal beat Millwall 2-0 when Brian Hill took charge.

sheets we have the players names and their numbers and colours.

2.20pm: We begin to get changed and the adrenalin starts flowing. We are all hoping it is going to be a good game.

2.40pm: We have a serious talk about the match and I give my match instructions to the linesmen and the reserve official.

2.55pm: I ring the ball to signal to the teams that it is time to go out on the field. The captains come to the middle for the toss-up and there is often a mascot. It's his big day and I like to make him feel part of things.

3.45pm: The first half is over and we are back in the changing room. There have been no real problems and we enjoy our cup of tea.

3.55pm: We are back out for the second half and that is perhaps slightly harder than the first half because the manager has had things to say to his players which may have got them even more fired up.

4.40pm: The game is over and we are coming off the pitch. It is nice when players come up to you and shake you by the hand and thank you.

4.45pm: We relax and have a shower and a cup of tea. We then deal with the paperwork by filling in substitutes on the team-sheets and logging the bookings.

5.30pm: We are changed and I thank the linesmen for their work and hope they have enjoyed the game. From there we go our own separate ways.

8.30pm: I arrive home and it's been a long day, almost 12 hours on the go. We certainly don't do it for the money, we do it for the enjoyment.

NOTTA LOTTA FANS KNOW THAT...

● **GARY CROSBY** (Nottingham Forest) and Manchester City's Andy Dibble (against whom Crosby headed last season's cheekiest and most controversial goal on March 3) share a birthday. On May 8, Crosby will be 27, Dibble 26.

Gary Crosbie scores after heading the ball out of 'keeper Dibble's hands ...

Newcastle's goalscoring ace Mick Quinn ... is a knockout!

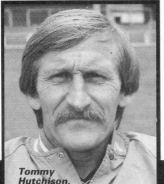
... when Andy thought he had it safely gathered.

● **STEVE BULL'S** first job, after leaving school, was in a bedding factory near Dudley.

INTERNATIONAL DOUBLE
● THERE ARE not many double internationals about these days, but Hibernian goalkeeper Andy Goram has played for Scotland at both soccer and cricket. He's brilliant at volleyball, too.

FAMOUS FANS
● ROY HUDD ... Crystal Palace; violinist Nigel Kennedy ... Aston Villa; Leslie Thomas ... Q.P.R.; Andy Peebles ... Manchester City; Tom Courtenay ... Hull City; Norman Wisdom ... Brighton; Richie Woodhall (light middleweight boxer who earned gold in the Commonwealth Games) ... W.B.A.

GOLDEN OLDIE
● OLDEST PLAYER in the Football League is Swansea City's 42-year-old player-coach Tommy Hutchison. Twenty-five years ago, Oldham gave the 17-year-old Hutchison a trial, then told him: "Sorry, son. You won't have the stamina for this game."

● **NEWCASTLE UNITED'S** top scorer has achieved the ultimate in popularity on Tyneside. He's had a pub drink named after him – the "Micky Quinn." They say it's a knock-out.

CRAZY DEBUTS
● PAUL GODDARD'S debuts for his three London clubs were all against Derby County – for Q.P.R., West Ham and, last season, for Millwall, following his £800,000 move FROM Derby.

Paul Goddard

Tommy Hutchison.

MUNRO MY TOP MAN

says his Rangers boss Souness

SUDDENLY everyone is singing the praises of the man they tagged the unsung hero of Ibrox.

Where recognition was once confined to the occasional pat on the back from manager Graeme Souness and quiet respect as a good pro, the impressive form of Stuart Munro has won over even the most critical of observers.

Last season he picked up a B&Q Skills Award as the top player in the Premier Division.

National team coach Andy Roxburgh then got in on the act by naming Munro in the Scotland side for the 'B' international against Yugoslavia.

And at Rangers supporters' clubs up and down the country, the notoriously hard-to-please Ibrox fans passed over all the big names in the team to honour their left-back as Player of the Year.

"Fame at last," joked the 27-year-old player. "Maybe I'm one of football's late developers.

"Seriously, I'm not too comfortable with all this attention. I prefer to do my job quietly, then fade into the background and let the likes of Mo Johnston and Ally McCoist get all the star treatment.

"I didn't let it get to me whenever I was on the receiving end of any stick so I've no intention of allowing myself to get carried away just because things are going well.

"Of course, it is nice to hear people say good things about me but at no time have I ever played to the crowd, the press or the cameras.

"Graeme Souness is the only man I've got to please so a simple nod of approval from him will always be more than enough to keep me happy."

Since he joined Rangers from Alloa Athletic just over six years ago - for the paltry sum of £35,000 - Stuart has been a model of consistency and it is indicative of his high level of performance that he has retained his place in the side despite the club's subsequent heavy investment in the transfer market.

Rangers have been linked with top quality players like Tony Dorigo, Stuart Pearce, Nigel Worthington and Colin Gibson, all of whom were tipped to fill the left-back berth, but the man in possession refused to let such speculation knock him out of his stride.

Indeed, he has seen off experienced men like Ally Dawson, Jimmy Phillips and Jan Bartram who had been earmarked for the number three shirt and he continues to hold down the job in the face of competition from squad colleagues John Brown, Tommy Cowan and Chris Vinnicombe.

Boss Graeme Souness makes absolutely no effort to conceal his admiration for the solid contribution made by Munro.

"The term 'model professional' tends to be over used these days," says Souness. "But it certainly applies to Stuart."

Tim (tracksuit) and Mark have a stab at one of the most gripping scenes.

When former Eastenders star Ross Davidson starred at their local Theatre Royal, Norwich City's Mark Bowen and Tim Sherwood couldn't resist getting in on the act...

Ross (centre) packed them in when he appeared in Wait Until Dark.

★STAGE

It was just plain murder when our two Canaries insisted on adding a touch of the macabre to the script.

Coming MON. 12th MARCH
NIGHTLY 8:00 · WED MAT 2:30 · SATURDAY 5 & 8

Pruneila Gee · Rodney Bewes
Peter Byrne · Ross Davidson in

WAIT UNTIL DARK

This World Famous Thriller by FREDERICK KNOTT

★ STRUCK

Ross explains the plot.

Ross relaxes with our scene-stealers before the curtain goes up.

Tim tries his hand at make-up.

'YOUNG CITIZENS'

Paul Lake sweeps past the Liverpool defence.

Another of the young Maine Road marvels ... Andy Hinchcliffe.

Ian Brightwell now established as a first team star.

Skipper Steve Redmond has set his sights on success.

David White has caught the eye.

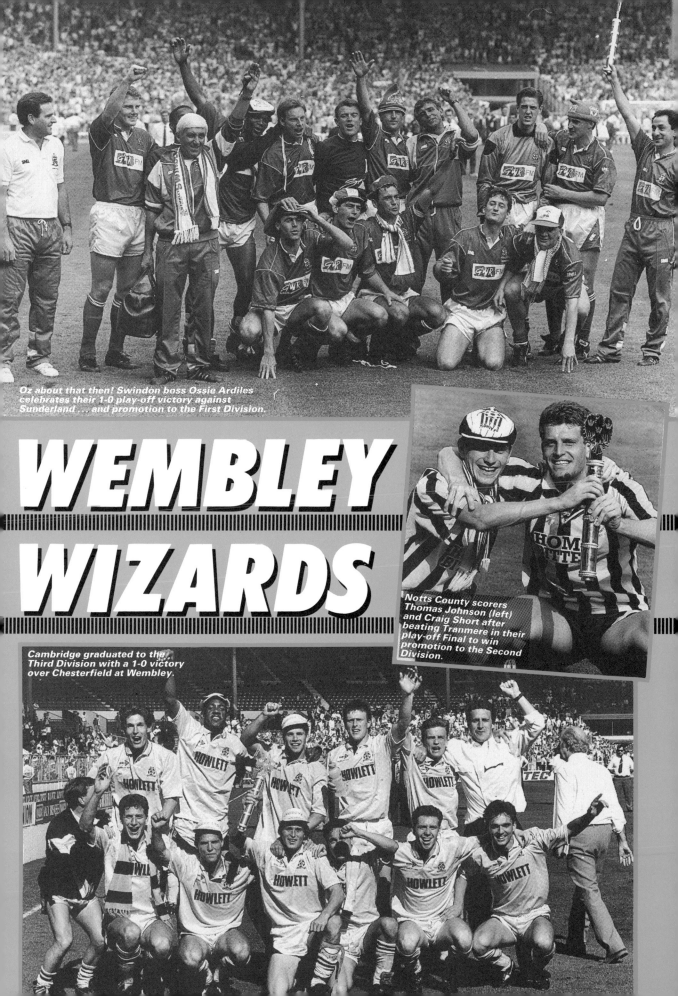

Oz about that then! Swindon boss Ossie Ardiles celebrates their 1-0 play-off victory against Sunderland . . . and promotion to the First Division.

WEMBLEY
WIZARDS

Notts County scorers Thomas Johnson (left) and Craig Short after beating Tranmere in their play-off Final to win promotion to the Second Division.

Cambridge graduated to the Third Division with a 1-0 victory over Chesterfield at Wembley.

KENNY DALGLISH This

Kenny's match-winner at Chelsea clinched the 1985-86 League Championship.

Footballer of the Year 1979.

YOU were born Kenny Mathieson Dalglish on March 4, 1951 in a block of Glasgow high-rise flats from where you can see Rangers' Ibrox Stadium.

As a boy you support Rangers but it is arch rivals Celtic who first spot your potential when a scout sees you playing for Glasgow United.

Assistant manager Sean Fallon calls at your house to invite you to sign for the Parkhead club and you remove the Rangers posters from your bedroom wall and sign for Celtic.

You make your League debut on October 4, 1969, at Raith and help Celtic to a 7-1 victory. In season 1971-72 you establish yourself in the first-team, scoring 17 goals in 31 League games.

Your achievements are recognised by your country on November 10, 1971 when Tommy Docherty awards you a first international cap, as a substitute against Belgium.

Docherty now says: "Kenny Dalglish is the sort of player I would like any youngster to model himself on."

That season ends with Celtic finishing as runners-up in the Premier

A ton-up performance for Scotland v Rumania in March 1986.

Hillsborough ... April 1989 ... one of the saddest days in British soccer history.

Division and winning the Scottish Cup.

The following term, Celtic win the League and are runners-up in both domestic Cup competitions, and a year later they enjoy even more success — winning the League and Cup double.

On November 26, 1974 you take part in probably your most important ever match — your marriage to Marina Harkins. Eleven months later, on October 3, 1975, your first daughter, Kelly, is born.

You succeed Billy McNeill as Celtic captain that season and lead the club to victory in both Cups. Your success story continues in 1976 when your 29 goals earn you Scotland's Player of the Year award.

The following year, 1977, is one of the most dramatic of your life. Once again, Celtic complete the double, your son Paul is born in March and in April, against Sweden, you captain Scotland for the first time.

is Your Life

On the way to scoring the goal that beat Bruges to win the European Cup in 1978.

In action for his beloved Celtic against Rangers.

But it is in August 1977 that you make the decision to leave Celtic and sign for Liverpool for a British record fee of £440,000.

Billy McNeill describes you as being "as near as you will ever get to the perfect player".

On your arrival at Anfield Bill Shankly tells you: "Don't over-eat and never lose your accent."

You score in your first six League games for Liverpool and at the end of your first season you score the only goal in the European Cup Final against FC Bruges at Wembley.

In 1979, you are voted Football Writers' Footballer of the Year and also help Liverpool win the League Championship. Liverpool regain the title the following season, 1980, and again in 1982, 1983 and 1984.

Your second daughter Lindsay is born in 1982 and in 1983 you are once more voted Football Writers' Footballer of the Year. The following year you receive the MBE.

In May 1985, only hours after the Heysel stadium tragedy, you are named as Liverpool's new manager, in succession to Joe Fagan. Many people are surprised by your appointment, but 12 months later, no-one doubts that it was the right decision.

In March you become the first player to win 100 caps for Scotland in the 3-0 win against Romania and on Saturday, May 3, at Stamford Bridge, you score the goal that clinches the First Division Championship.

The following Friday, you are named Bells Manager of the Year and on

Celebrating the Double in his first season as player-manager.

Saturday, May 10, you are part of the Liverpool team that beats Everton in the FA Cup Final and so become the first player-manager to win the double.

In the 1987-88 season Liverpool put together an astonishing sequence of 29 League games without defeat from the start of the season and, in February, daughter Lauren becomes another addition to the family.

The title is duly won and you are only denied a second double by Lawrie Sanchez's winner for Wimbledon in the FA Cup Final.

Emotional

The next season sees the FA Cup back at Anfield, after an emotional victory over Everton, but the League title is snatched from your grasp in the last seconds of the season by Arsenal, for whom Michael Thomas is the goalscoring hero.

You put the record straight by steering The Reds to their 18th title triumph last season, making your first appearance in two years in the last home game of the season against Derby.

It is also your last appearance as a player when you come on as a second-half substitute.

Liverpool win 1-0, thanks to a late goal by Gary Gillespie. You receive the Barclays League Championship trophy after the game to bow out as a player in true Liverpool style.

A couple of weeks later, you receive the Barclays Manager of the Year Award … a fitting tribute to another fine season.

No-one doubts there will be more honours to come….

Kenny Dalglish…This Is Your Life!

Tony with
Lyndsey and
son Anthony.

'Bonzo m

happy

WEST HAM defender Tony Gale is one of the nicest guys you could wish to meet.

A dedicated professional … happy family man … tremendous personality and great company.

Then, suddenly last season he became withdrawn. Gone was one of the famous smiles in football.

Tony's performances on the field suffered. He looked tense … tackles were mistimed … passes went astray … the head went down. He was clearly unhappy.

It was as though a sudden whirlwind had sucked up the Tony Gale we all loved and dumped another person in his place.

The cause of the depression was easy to diagnose … the appointment of Lou Macari by newly relegated West Ham in July 1989 to replace the long-serving John Lyall.

"I know John was very popular at the club, but don't think we were all against Lou Macari from the start because we weren't," says Tony.

"We were all prepared to support him and have a real go at getting back into the First Division.

"But it soon became apparent that the style of play Lou wanted wasn't what I, or West Ham, had been used to and enjoyed.

"Lou didn't want us playing from the back. His objective was to get the ball upfield as quickly as possible.

"The big boot is not my game and it was made clear by Lou's team

Rock bottom … West Ham's 6-0 Littlewoods Cup Semi-Final defeat at Oldham.

de Hammers again'

Upton Park favourite ... Billy Bonds.

selections that I had no future at the club.

"It was as though a great storm cloud had descended over Upton Park. Suddenly the club was making headlines for all the wrong reasons.

"Then in a Littlewoods Cup Semi-Final first-leg tie at Oldham in February, The Hammers hit rock-bottom.

"We were thrashed 6-0 ... and deservedly so. The team couldn't even put part of the blame on the plastic pitch.

"It was a dreadful performance, the worst of my career. We had let down ourselves, the club and the thousands of wonderful fans who had travelled to Oldham on a freezing, wet and windy night."

Hectic

Added to his problems on the field, Tony's wife Lyndsey had given birth to daughter Alexandra and there were serious complications.

Tony was dashing home from training straight to the hospital where his new daughter was in special care.

"Lyndsey was great, so was my mum, dad and the rest of my large family," says Tony.

"Friends and team-mates were also very supportive, especially Phil Parkes who was busy with his Testimonial Year."

Then, sensation! Lou Macari, the subject of an alleged betting scandal at his previous club Swindon resigned in the best interests of West Ham.

Hammer hero Billy Bonds was promoted from youth team coach to manager with another of the Upton Park faithful Ronnie Boyce, as his assistant.

Suddenly, the storm clouds were blown away like the bubbles in West Ham's famous club song.

"Stability was restored to the whole club," says Galey.

"The whole atmosphere changed. There were over 20,000 at Bonzo's first game, a home match against Blackburn.

"The reception Bonzo and the team received was unbelievable. We knew the fans were right behind us again. West Ham United were a family again.

"Although the game ended 1-1, we outplayed Rovers and should have slaughtered them.

"On reflection, the two points

dropped, and the two missed penalties against Port Vale a month later, probably cost us promotion."

After the Blackburn game, Hammers drew 2-2 with Port Vale and won seven at home.

And that included a tremendous 3-0 victory over Oldham in the second-leg of their Littlewoods Cup-tie.

So, was Tony disappointed West Ham just missed out on a place in the play-offs last season ... and with it a chance of a quick return to the First Division?

"Obviously we all wanted to get back and Bonzo had to go for it. But maybe it will turn out to be a blessing in disguise. Now at least Billy will have some time to consolidate and strengthen the squad.

Surely Lou Macari did that, buying Trevor Morley and Ian Bishop from Manchester City, Jimmy Quinn from Bradford, Colin Foster from Nottingham Forest, Martin Allen from QPR and bringing over the Czechoslovakia 'keeper Ludek Miklosko?

"Yes, I must praise Lou for his signings, they have all done well for West Ham and should play a vital part of our progress this season.

"Although the Second Division is a tough one again, with as many as ten clubs likely to be in contention for the First, West Ham are aiming for the top two."

With the likes of Newcastle, Sheffield Wednesday, Oldham, Millwall, Charlton and Ipswich (now managed by John Lyall) around, every game will be like a Cup-tie to West Ham.

"This should prove an advantage because as they have proved so often in the past ... the bigger the game, the higher The Hammers will rise to the occasion," says Tony, signing off with one of his customary cheeky grins.

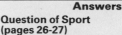

Lou Macari.

John Lyall.

West Germany star Pierre Littbarski admires the adidas ball.

The

When the World Cup Finals kicked-off in Italy on June 8th we couldn't possibly have known exactly how many goals would have been scored. But we did know for certain that every goal scored would be with the 'Etrusco Unico'.

That was the official tournament ball, supplied and developed specially for Italia 90 by adidas.

Probably the last thing on your mind as you sat watching the action from Italy, was the thought that the balls stroked around by the world's elite group of soccer stars had cost millions of pounds to develop in to an unrivalled finished product.

The balls were put through a rigourous set of tests with the help of international research institutes and numerous top club sides in Europe and South America. The durability of the ball and it's outer coating for example, was tested by firing it against a hard surface at an amazing 200 km/hour in cycles of 400, 800, 1,600, 3,200 and 4,800 times.

Then the balls were fully submerged under water for long

The Azteca ball was used for the 1986 World Cup Finals in Mexico.

Ball Game

periods and only those whose weight and therefore playing characteristics did not alter passed the test. It was also found that the synthetic material used for the 'Etrusco Unico' is far better than leather – for years the traditional football material.

And the result of all these tests was a ball totally waterproof, true and perfect for the long-range power play of the world's top players. As West Germany's brilliant winger Pierre Littbarski says: 'With the new ball at your feet you feel like a South American player. It is so easy to control!"

Even the name 'Etrusco Unico' wasn't decided in a hurry. It was inspired by an ancient Italian people, the Etruscans, whose culture was based around art, sporting competitions and hunting, long before the Roman era began.

And now it is adidas who are making history as they lead the world in football manufacturing, carrying on a tradition for supplying the top balls for the top tournaments just as they did in the previous Mexican World Cup with the 'Azteca Mexico'.

OFFICIAL BALL
OF THE FIFA
WORLD CUP
1990

Left: England's Gary Lineker won a Golden Shoe Award for being top scorer in the 1986 World Cup Finals. Argentina's Maradona also won an adidas award for being voted the Player of the 1986 World Cup Finals.

Reds romp home in the G

What a goal! Ian Rush celebrates scoring Liverpool's second goal against Everton.

A special SHOOT spotlight on the Football League scoring records of the 1980's, and guess what? Liverpool came out on top!

UNDISPUTED Champions of English football Liverpool are also the tops when it comes to scoring goals.

During the last ten seasons they plundered a staggering 755 goals in the League alone – 69 more than their nearest rivals Sheffield United.

The consistency of the mighty Reds has to be admired and a glance at our exclusive table from 1980-81–1989-90 shows how their strike rate varies little from season-to-season.

When you consider that the majority of the teams in the League have played more games than Liverpool their achievement is all the more remarkable.

The Blades of Sheffield figure prominently in the race along with

The Goalden Boys

1	Liverpool	62	80	87	73	68	89	72	87	65	78	765
2	Sheffield Utd	65	94	62	86	54	64	50	45	93	78	691
3	Swindon	51	55	61	58	62	82	77	73	68	79	666
4	Colchester	45	82	75	69	87	88	64	47	60	48	665
5	Northampton	65	57	65	53	53	79	103	70	66	51	662
6	Bury	70	80	74	61	76	63	54	58	55	70	661
7	Wimbledon	64	61	96	97	71	58	57	58	50	47	659
8	York	37	69	88	96	70	77	55	48	62	55	657
9	Scunthorpe	60	43	71	54	83	50	73	76	77	69	656
10	Reading	62	67	64	84	68	67	52	44	68	77	653
11	Chelsea	46	60	51	90	63	57	53	50	96	58	646
12	Spurs	70	67	65	64	78	74	68	38	60	60	644
12	Watford	50	76	74	68	81	69	67	27	74	58	644
14	Bradford	53	88	68	73	77	50	62	74	52	44	641
15	Gillingham	48	64	58	74	80	81	65	77	47	46	640
15	Orient	52	36	64	71	51	79	64	85	86	52	640
15	Southend	78	63	66	55	58	69	78	65	56	51	640
18	Wigan	51	80	60	46	60	82	83	70	55	48	635
19	Brentford	52	56	88	69	62	58	64	53	66	66	634
20	Port Vale	57	56	67	51	61	67	76	58	78	62	633
21	Tranmere	59	51	49	53	83	74	54	61	62	86	632
21	Everton	55	56	66	44	88	87	76	53	50	73	632
23	Notts County	49	61	55	50	45	71	77	82	64	77	631
24	Blackpool	45	66	55	70	73	66	74	71	56	49	625
25	Fulham	57	77	64	60	68	45	59	69	69	55	623
26	Exeter	62	71	81	50	57	47	53	53	65	83	622
27	Walsall	59	51	64	68	58	90	80	68	41	40	619
28	Bristol Rovers	34	58	86	68	66	51	49	68	67	71	618
29	Oxford	39	63	71	91	84	62	44	44	62	57	617
29	Plymouth	55	56	61	56	62	88	62	65	55	58	617
31	Southampton	76	72	54	66	56	51	69	49	52	71	616
32	Bristol City	29	40	59	70	74	69	63	77	53	76	610
33	Ipswich	77	75	64	55	46	32	59	61	71	67	607
33	West Ham	79	66	68	60	51	74	52	40	37	80	607
35	Wrexham	43	40	56	59	49	68	72	69	77	70	603
36	Leicester	40	56	72	65	65	54	54	62	56	77	601
37	Portsmouth	55	56	74	73	69	69	53	36	53	62	600
38	Man. United	51	59	56	71	77	70	52	71	45	46	598
39	Hull	40	70	75	71	78	65	41	54	45	58	597
39	Nott'm For	62	42	62	76	56	69	64	67	44	55	597
41	Peterborough	68	71	58	72	54	52	57	52	52	59	595
41	Bournemouth	47	62	59	63	57	65	76	56	53	57	595
43	Arsenal	61	48	58	74	61	49	58	58	73	54	594
44	Rotherham	62	66	45	57	55	61	48	50	76	71	591
45	Huddersfield	71	64	84	56	52	43	54	41	63	61	589
46	Preston	41	50	60	66	51	54	72	48	79	65	586

124

REAT GOALS RACE

Swindon Town. But take a look at the team in fourth place.

Colchester United, now in the Vauxhall Conference after a disastrous 1989-90 season, managed 665 goals before losing their League status.

At the bottom end of the table, it's no surprise to see Newport propping up the rest. Here's how the 92 clubs finished:—

Above: Tony Agana hits Sheffield United's second in a 4-1 win v Watford.

Left: Swindon's Steve Foley heads home in their 2-1 away victory at West Brom.

The Goalden Boys

47	Burnley	60	66	56	76	60	60	53	57	52	45	585	70	Sheff. Wed.	53	55	60	72	58	63	58	52	34	35	540
48	Blackburn	42	47	58	57	66	53	45	68	74	74	584	70	Carlisle	56	65	68	48	50	43	39	57	53	61	540
48	Aldershot	43	57	61	76	56	66	64	64	48	49	584	72	Rochdale	60	50	55	52	55	57	54	47	56	52	538
50	Newcastle	30	52	74	85	55	67	47	55	32	80	577	73	Sunderland	52	38	48	42	40	45	49	92	60	70	536
51	Aston Villa	72	55	62	59	60	51	45	68	45	57	574	73	Chester	38	36	55	45	60	83	61	51	64	43	536
52	Oldham	39	50	64	47	49	52	65	72	75	59	572	75	Grimsby	44	53	45	60	72	47	39	48	55	70	533
52	Luton	61	86	65	53	57	61	47	57	42	43	572	76	Derby	57	53	49	36	75	80	64	35	40	43	532
54	Doncaster	59	55	57	82	72	45	56	40	49	53	568	76	Darlington	65	61	61	49	66	61	45	71	53	VC	532
55	Chesterfield	72	57	43	59	64	61	56	41	51	63	567	78	West Brom	60	46	51	48	58	35	51	50	65	67	531
55	Wolves	42	32	68	27	37	57	69	71	96	67	567	79	Lincoln	66	66	77	59	50	55	45	VC	64	48	530
57	Hartlepool	64	73	46	47	55	68	44	50	50	66	563	79	Cambridge	53	48	42	28	37	65	60	50	71	76	530
57	Man. City	56	49	47	66	66	43	36	80	77	43	563	81	Norwich	49	64	52	48	46	84	53	40	48	44	528
59	Mansfield	58	63	61	66	41	74	52	48	48	60	561	82	Cardiff	44	45	76	53	47	53	48	66	44	51	527
59	Millwall	43	62	64	71	73	50	40	72	47	39	561	83	Swansea	64	58	51	36	53	43	56	62	51	45	519
59	Halifax	44	51	59	56	42	70	59	54	69	57	561	83	C. Palace	47	34	43	42	46	57	51	86	71	42	519
62	Hereford	38	64	42	54	65	74	60	41	66	56	560	85	Torquay	55	47	56	59	38	43	56	66	45	53	518
63	QPR	56	65	77	67	53	53	48	48	43	45	555	86	Charlton	63	50	63	53	51	78	45	38	44	31	516
64	Barnsley	72	61	57	57	42	37	49	61	66	49	551	87	Coventry	47	56	48	57	47	48	50	46	47	40	486
64	Leeds	39	39	51	55	66	44	58	61	59	79	551	88	Middlesbro	53	34	46	41	41	44	67	63	44	52	485
66	Bolton	61	39	42	56	69	54	46	66	58	59	550	89	Shrewsbury	46	37	48	49	66	43	41	42	37	76	485
67	Crewe	48	29	53	56	55	54	70	57	67	56	545	90	Stoke	51	44	53	44	24	40	63	50	57	35	461
68	Stockport	44	48	60	60	58	63	40	44	54	73	544	91	Birmingham	50	53	40	39	59	30	47	41	31	60	450
69	Brighton	54	43	38	69	54	64	37	69	57	56	541	92	Newport	64	54	76	58	55	52	49	35	VC	–	443

*Maidstone not included
VC – Vauxhall Conference